Fr. Robert J. Kus

FLOWERS IN THE WIND 5

MORE STORY~BASED HOMILIES FOR CYCLE B

RED LANTERN PRESS
WILMINGTON, NORTH CAROLINA

www.redlanternpress.com

Books by Red Lantern Press

Journals by Fr. Robert J. Kus

- Dreams for the Vineyard: Journal of a Parish Priest - 2002

- For Where Your Treasure Is: Journal of a Parish Priest – 2003

- There Will Your Heart Be Also: Journal of a Parish Priest – 2004

- Field of Plenty: Journal of a Parish Priest – 2005

- Called to the Coast: Journal of a Parish Priest – 2006

- Then Along Came Marcelino: Journal of a Parish Priest – 2007

- Living the Dream: Journal of a Parish Priest - 2008

- A Hand to Honduras: Journal of a Parish Priest – 2009

- Beacon of Hope: Journal of a Parish Priest - 2010

Homily Collections by Fr. Robert J. Kus

- Flowers in the Wind 1 – Story-Based Homilies for Cycle B

- Flowers in the Wind 2 – Story-Based Homilies for Cycle C

- Flowers in the Wind 3 – Story-Based Homilies for Cycle A

- Flowers in the Wind 4 – *More* Story-Based Homilies for Cycle A

- Flowers in the Wind 5 – *More* Story-Based Homilies for Cycle B

ISBN-13: 9781519129161
ISBN-10: 1519129165

Dedication

In Loving Memory of My Grandparents

Theodore (Sr.) & Marcella Kus

Of

Maple Heights, Ohio

Acknowledgements

Many thanks go to Nolan Heath and Pat Marriott of the Basilica Shrine of St. Mary in Wilmington, N.C. who helped with the editing of these homilies.

Many thanks also go to the parishioners of both St. Catherine of Siena Parish in Wake Forest, N.C. and the Basilica Shrine of St. Mary for whom I originally created these homilies.

Thanks also go to the fine folks at Createspace who always do their best to assist whenever needed.

Table of Contents

Introduction

TABLE OF CONTENTS

Introduction

The purpose of this book is to provide Catholic preachers a complete second collection of Sunday (& Christmas) homilies for Cycle B. Though it is designed specifically for Catholic priests and deacons, the homilies should prove useful for preachers in other mainstream Christian denominations as well.

Each homily starts with the Sunday of the Year being celebrated followed by the Scripture selection that is being discussed. This is followed by a story that appeals for people of all ages. Finally, each homily then discusses the concepts that can be gleaned from the Scripture and story and how we can apply them to our everyday lives.

Each homily takes less than eight minutes. This is especially important for preachers who are in parishes that have Masses every 90 minutes and have to get parking lots filled and emptied in a limited amount of time.

The homilies were created while I was pastor of parishes with large concentrations of children. I'm happy to say the stories make the homilies vibrant and interesting, and families love talking about the stories during the week.

Preachers may take the homilies whole, or they may tweak them to fit their specific needs.

Every effort has been made to credit the authors of each story. In the event that this was not possible, the story sources are listed as being written by "Anonymous."

Part One

ADVENT &
CHRISTMAS SEASONS

Chapter 1

1st Sunday of Advent - B
Swimming the Channel

Scripture:

- Isaiah 63: 16b-17, 19b; 64: 2-7
- Psalm 80: 2ac & 3b, 15-16, 18-19
- 1 Corinthians 1: 3-9
- Mark 13: 33-37

Today, Catholic Christians begin a new liturgical year with the 4-week season of Advent, the season of "joyful expectation." In this new church year, the Sunday Gospels will primarily be from the Gospel of Mark.

Most Bible scholars today believe that the Gospel of Mark is the oldest of the Gospels, and that the writers of the Gospels of Matthew and Luke borrowed many of their ideas from two books: the Gospel of Mark, and a book they simply call "Q."

Bible scholars also reject the idea that the author of the Gospel of Mark was actually a person named "Mark." Rather, they believe that an anonymous writer created this book from stories and ideas and sayings of Jesus and put them together in a book.

For our purposes, it is not important to know the name of the writer of the Gospel. Rather, like all books of the Bible, we are to glean the important messages and put them into practice in our lives.

The first two weeks of Advent focus on waiting for Jesus at the end of time, and the second two weeks focus on waiting for Jesus as the Christ Child.

In today's Gospel selection, we hear Jesus reminding us emphatically about our own mortality when he says, "Be watchful! Be alert! You do not know when the time will come" (Mark 13: 33).

The message that Jesus wants us to grasp is that heaven is our goal. All of the things we experience on our journeys in this life are fleeting. Heaven, therefore, should always be our primary goal.

Unfortunately, sometimes we take our eyes off the goal. We become distracted. When that happens, we fail in our journey. That is what happened to the woman in the following story.

The story begins on Santa Catalina Island, twenty-one miles from the coast of California. A 34-year-old long-distance swimmer named Florence Chadwick decided to swim the channel between the island and the coast. Now, Florence was not an amateur. On the contrary, she had already swum the English Channel in both directions. She was now determined to be the first woman in history to swim the Catalina Channel.

On July 4, 1952, Florence began to swim from Santa Catalina Island to the California coast. Unfortunately for her, however, it was a very foggy day. Hour after hour, Florence kept swimming. She battled cold and fatigue, and many times sharks threatened her safety. She kept trying to see the shore, but because of the dense fog, she was not able to see the shore. Finally, after fifteen hours and fifty-five minutes, Florence decided she could no longer continue. Rescue boats took her safely to shore.

When she returned to shore, Florence was shocked to learn that she had been only a half-mile from the coast. She told a reporter, "Look, I'm not excusing myself, but if I could have seen land, I know I could have made it." Florence learned that she had not been defeated by cold or fatigue. Rather, the fog had defeated her, for it had obscured her goal. The fog had blinded her eyes, her reason, and most importantly, her spirit.

Two months later, Florence Chadwick swam the same channel, and again the fog blocked her vision. This time, however, Florence remembered that no matter how much the fog blocked her vision, somewhere beyond it was the coast. This time, Florence succeeded. Not only was she the first woman to swim the Catalina Channel, she beat the men's record by two hours.

In examining the Gospel passage and the story of Florence Chadwick, we learn the importance of keeping our focus on the end goal. There are three things, in particular, that can lead us to lose sight of our ultimate heavenly goal.

First, some people may fail to reach personal goals in life and, therefore, begin to think God doesn't care about them. This, then, leads some to abandon their faith or religious practices. I have seen this many times with men who want to become priests or deacons or brothers. They apply for acceptance into a religious community or diocese, and when they don't get accepted, they drift away from the Church, the sacraments, and prayer.

Second, some lose sight of their heavenly goal because of a tragedy in life. They experience something devastating, and begin to think God hates them or is punishing them or doesn't care about them. Sometimes, this happens to people who lose a loved one or their health. Unlike many who grow from tragedy, these folks are crushed by it.

And third, addictions can lead people to abandon their faith and religious practices. These addictions could be to mind-altering drugs such as alcohol, cocaine, or heroin. The addictions could be to sex or gambling. Or, more frequently, people frequently get addicted to the things of the world, falling into the deadly spiritual disorder known as materialism. Materialism is most likely to show up in rich societies such as the United States where people are surrounded by every material item imaginable.

As we continue our life journeys this week, it would be a good idea to reflect on our own lives. Are there any dangers lurking in our lives that prevent us from keeping our eyes on our ultimate goal – getting to heaven?

And that is the good news I have for you on this First Sunday of Advent.

Story source: Anonymous, "Never Lose Sight of Goals," in Brian Cavanaugh (Ed.), *Fresh Packet of Sower's Seeds: Third Planting*. Mahwah, N.J.: Paulist Press, 1994, #41, pp. 36-37.

Chapter 2

2nd Sunday of Advent - B
Lunch with Grandma

Scripture:

- Isaiah 40: 1-5, 9-11
- Psalm 85: 9ab & 10, 11-12, 13-14
- 2 Peter 3: 8-14
- Mark 1: 1-8

Today, Catholic Christians celebrate the Second Sunday of Advent. As we remember from last week, the first two weeks of Advent encourage us to remember life after life, that is, the coming of Jesus at the end of time. The second two weeks of Advent are devoted to waiting for Jesus as the Christ Child.

Today, the author of the Second Letter of Peter tells us that the Lord does not want us to perish, but that we should all come to repentance (2 Peter 3: 9). The author then goes on to say, "But the day of the Lord will come like a thief, and then the heavens will pass away with a mighty roar and the elements will be dissolved by fire, and the earth and everything done on it will be found out. Since everything is to be dissolved in this way, what sort of persons ought you to be, conducting yourselves in holiness and devotion" (2 Peter 3: 10-11). "Therefore, beloved, since you await these things, be eager to be found without spot or blemish before him, at peace" (2 Peter 3: 14).

Sometimes, people read passages like this and come to the conclusion that if they were truly living their lives in holiness, all would be wonderful. Their lives would be peaceful. Everything they did would turn out great. Their businesses would flourish, their families would be problem-free, and they would glide though life like carefree angels. These are the people who mistake the concept of "fruits" – as in "by their fruits you shall know them" – with results.

Actually, the "fruits" that the Scriptures tell us about are not the consequences of our actions. Rather, they refer to our actions themselves. Sometimes our actions turn out great. Other times, they turn out badly. What we are being judged on is not the consequences of the actions, but the actions themselves. That is what the young woman in the following story discovered.

There was once a young woman named Teri Batts. She had a grandmother in Charlotte who was suffering from Alzheimer's disease. Her grandmother lived with Teri's mother.

One day, Teri came to Charlotte to visit her mother and grandmother. Although she was a very upbeat, positive, enthusiastic person, she was quite unprepared and unaware of the challenges of working with a person with Alzheimer's disease. For example, before she even had her first cup of coffee, she found her Grandma in the bathroom trying to brush her teeth with a razor blade. Frantically, Teri called out for help. Teri's mother calmly walked in and took the razor blade from Grandma.

A couple of days passed, and Teri began to become more comfortable and confident being around her disabled Grandma. Teri and her mother noted, for example, that grandma was a creature of habit. Therefore, they would mess up the living room so that Grandma could straighten it up again and again, having her sweep the porch, and washing unbreakable plates and cups as Teri dried them and put them away.

After a few more days, Teri felt confident enough to take Grandma to a restaurant for lunch. Though this was against her mother's better judgment, Teri decided to take grandma to a steakhouse that had a large salad bar. She reasoned that Grandma would appreciate being able to pick out food she liked, instead of always being served things that others chose for her.

Unfortunately, when they got to the salad bar, the only thing Grandma recognized was the "red stuff that wiggled" – gelatin. So, that is the only thing she chose to eat.

All was going well at the table when, suddenly, Grandma grabbed Teri's arm and yanked her to the floor, pulling her under the table. When Teri tried to get her to come out from under the table, Grandma told her there were "Indians!" She quietly said, "We must escape."

When Teri asked where the Indians were, Grandma pointed to a group of people who had just entered the restaurant. Grandma commanded Teri to crawl between the tables, imagining this to be a Wild West saloon. Grandma kept looking from side to side for an Indian attack while she dragged her purse behind her.

When the manager came from behind the counter, Grandma flung herself over Teri's body to protect her. When the manager gazed down on the two piled up on the floor, he asked, "Can I help you ladies?"

At that, Teri burst out laughing. She laughed so hard, that she couldn't stand. At that moment, Grandma brushed Teri off and asked, "Are you okay, honey?"

The confused manager asked the obvious question, "Is anything wrong?"

Grandma, who thought she was in an episode of the television western, *Gunsmoke*, replied, "Of course, everything is quite all right now that you are here, Marshall Dillon."

Teri had tears of hysterical laughter streaming down her face when Grandma turned back to the manager and said, "I'm sorry, sir, we forgot to pay." With that, she took a dime out of her purse and put it on the counter.

"Thank you, ma'am," said the manager and gave her a big smile.

By now, Teri was laughing so hard she could hardly breathe. Grandma gripped Teri's arm and jerked her to the door. "We have to get out of here, Teri, you're embarrassing me."

And as God watched from heaven above, all he saw was Teri's love and care. He ignored the fiasco that ensued. That's how God is. He only judges our actions, not how they turn out.

And that is the good news I have for you on this Second Sunday of Advent.

"Lunch with Grandma," by Teri Batts, in Jack Canfield & Mark Victor Hansen (Edited by Amy Newmark), *Chicken Soup for the Soul: Older & Wiser*, Cos Cob, Connecticut: Chicken Soup for the Soul Publishing, LLC, 2008, pp. 253-255.

Chapter 3

3rd Sunday of Advent - B
Thanksgiving in Prison

Scripture:

* Isaiah 61: 1-2a, 10-11
* Luke 1: 46-48, 49-50, 53-54
* 1 Thessalonians 5: 16-24
* John 1: 6-8, 19-28

Today, Catholic Christians celebrate the Third Sunday of Advent, sometimes known as Gaudete Sunday, the Sunday of Joy. It is one of only two Sundays of the church year when the priest may wear rose-colored vestments. This is the week when we light the rose-colored candle on our Advent wreaths.

Today's Scripture readings have many themes that we could explore. In this homily, however, we will focus on a Christian commandment that is found in St. Paul's First Letter to the Thessalonians. The commandment is this: "In all circumstances give thanks, for this is the will of God for you in Christ Jesus" (1 Thessalonians 5: 18).

It is easy to give thanks to God in the times of our lives when everything is going well. But the Christian commandment we encounter today says we are to give thanks in all circumstances. "All" means "all," in bad times as well as in good times.

One man who appears to have grasped this concept is Mark Land. He wrote the following essay while he was experiencing a dark time in his life as a prisoner in Indiana. The essay is called "Being Thankful on Thanksgiving Day in Federal Prison Camp."

> As I rise this morning and am preparing for Thanksgiving Day on Thursday, I begin my morning, like all other mornings, giving thanks to the Lord for all of the blessings that I have. I am so grateful for all of the extraordinary blessings that I have in life. A forgiving God, a beautiful partner, an amazing family, people who love and support me and on and on.......I am thankful for all of the wonderful blessings that I have in my life. Even those of us in the worst of circumstances can find many things to be grateful for this Thanksgiving. In a world with increasing tensions and chaos, full of greed and corruption, we must try to find peace and gratitude in our heart this holiday season. You can find rest in the peace of the Lord. In 5 short months I will be released back to society a very different man. I will dedicate the rest of my life helping others overcome the obstacles associated with enduring great adversity in life. Thriving through adversity is

a CHOICE. You can CHOOSE to lie down or get back up. I live by the motto: "Fall 7 times, get back up 8." It is not easy and is definitely the road chosen by very few. Being thankful each and every day, not just during the holiday season, is one of the most important elements of surviving and thriving during difficult times. My mother used to say: "God never promised us a rose garden." Life is far from perfect. During this special time of year we must analyze and take inventory of our lives and identify the beauty that often goes unnoticed or is neglected on a daily basis. Next summer I will release a book about my observations from Federal Prison and how to live a life of integrity and honesty in a world today where corruption and greed is not only ACCEPTED, but also glorified and encouraged. Federal Prison saved my life. I am grateful for those who gave me this burden. They did me a tremendous favor. Choosing to live today with honesty, integrity and maintaining a high standard of ETHICS is not easy, but it is the only way to find peace and joy. I recently had to explain to my 14 year old son how bad choices have bad consequences. WE CHOOSE OUR OWN DESTINY IN LIFE. IT IS A CHOICE. CHOOSE GOODNESS AT ALL TIMES IN EVERYTHING YOU DO, AND YOU WILL BE BLESSED IN WAYS YOU COULD NEVER IMAGINE. May all of you have a Blessed Thanksgiving AND may the peace of our Lord bring you joy and happiness during this holiday season.

Giving thanks to God is a commandment that is easy to fulfill in good times, and harder to fulfill in bad times. Nevertheless, we are to give thanks "in all circumstances." Some people make "giving thanks" too complicated. They confuse "giving thanks" with an emotional response. That, however, is false. Giving thanks is an act of the will, not of the emotions. A prayer such as "Thank you God for watching over me" is one that we can say in any circumstances. We can say it when we feel good or feel miserable. Our feeling states should not matter in thanking God.

As we continue our life journeys this week, it would be a good idea to reflect on our own lives. How do we thank God each and every day for loving us and watching over us?

And that is the good news I have for you on this Third Sunday of Advent.

Story source: "Being thankful on Thanksgiving Day in Federal Prison Camp" by Mark Land. Www.EticaLLC, Nov. 25, 2014.

Chapter 4

4th Sunday of Advent - B
Green Trees of Winter

Scripture:

- 2 Samuel 7: 1-5, 8b-12, 14a, 16
- Psalm 89: 2-3, 4-5, 27 & 29
- Romans 16: 25-27
- Luke 1: 26-38

Today, Catholic Christians celebrate the Fourth Sunday of Advent. On this day, we hear the story of the Angel Gabriel coming to visit Mary. He told Mary that she was going to become pregnant by the Holy Spirit, bear a son, and call him Jesus. Though Mary was baffled by all of this, she simply said, "Behold, I am the handmaid of the Lord. May it be done to me according to your word" (Luke 1: 38).

God calls each of us to serve him in this life in some way. But, God doesn't send us angels to tell us what to do with our lives, as he did in Mary's case.

God does, however, send us clues to guide us. But before we examine these clues, we have to be aware of what gifts God has given us, and we need to be satisfied with what we have. If we don't accept ourselves, we can't be at peace, and without peace, we will continually be in conflict. That is what we see in the following Algonquian Indian vocation story that discusses why only certain trees stay green in the winter.

Many years ago, the Great Spirit allowed all creatures to roam the earth. Just as the elk and deer and bears roamed freely, so did the trees. The trees could walk around to search for water, enjoy sunshine, or seek the shade of the mountains when the sun was too hot for them.

Unlike the deer and rabbits, though, the trees could only move slowly. They would roam the earth in the spring, summer, and autumn, and then rest in the winter.

One day, however, the trees began to argue among themselves. They became jealous of each other. The elm wanted the hillside to itself, and the poplar wanted the valley where the oak was. The hickory trees wanted to be by the stream where the beech trees liked to hang out. Only the trees with pointy needles, such as the pines and firs, were satisfied.

The Great Spirit was not at all happy with the complaining trees. After sending thunder to get their attention, the Great Spirit said, "I have given you life and the beauty of your leaves and fruit, and the ability to roam the earth, and you are not satisfied!"

The Great Spirit then told the trees, "From this day on, you will be rooted in the ground and not be able to move freely on the earth any more. Only your seeds will be able to move around. You will lose your leaves in the winter and shiver in the cold and ice and snow. That is because you have not been satisfied with what I have given you. Only the gentle pines, cedars, spruce and firs will keep their tiny green leaves throughout the year, and they shall forever be called evergreens. They will grow straight and tall, and they will be the ones who shall hold their heads above all the other trees in the forest."

And so it came to pass many years ago. To this day, many people claim that when they walk through the forest in the winter, they can hear the moaning of the trees that have lost their leaves as they shiver in the cold, waiting for the spring.

This beautiful story reminds us that each of us has different gifts or talents, and we should be grateful for what God has given us. If we are ungrateful, we cannot live in peace. That would be a miserable life indeed.

Now before discussing three ways to discern what God wants us to do with our lives, we need to first remember that we have been called to be Catholic Christians. That is our primary vocation. This homily, though, is more about how we figure out the other parts of our lives.

First, we need to take stock of what God has given us to work with. These gifts include all of the elements that make us who we are. Only when we identify these can we be fully aware of our qualifications for vocational paths. God, for example, has not given me the necessary requirements to be a Harlem Globetrotter or an Indian chief. That's fine with me, though, because I never wanted to be either of those things.

Second, we need to pay attention to the desires that God has planted in our hearts. Desires are the most important clues. But some desires are so strong that people don't even identify them. This is seen in many people who get married. They never even considered a life outside of the married state. If you asked them how they knew God was calling them to the married state, they would probably give you a blank stare. They never even considered the desire to get married as a vocational clue, or marriage as a vocational decision.

God gives these clues also for our occupational journeys. If you ever watched the television show *The Waltons*, for example, you saw how the desire to fly was planted in Jim Bob's heart, the desire to write planted in John Boy's heart, and the desire to be a nurse and physician planted in Mary Ellen's heart.

And third, we need to examine these desires and ask ourselves two basic questions. One, am I willing to pay the cost to make these desires a reality? And two, do I have the necessary requirements to make these desires come true? If you're not willing to spend a minimum of 8 years of study following high school to become a priest, for example, you might want to rule out priesthood. And if you lack the necessary intelligence to become a rocket scientist, it would be good to rule that out.

The important thing to remember is that no matter what we do occupationally with our lives, we should strive to serve the Lord the best we can all the days of our lives.

And that is the good news I have for you on this Fourth Sunday of Advent.

Story source: Anonymous, "Legend of the Trees," in Brian Cavanaugh (Ed.'s) *The Sower's Seeds*, Mahwah, N.J.: Paulist Press, 1990, #63, pp. 50-51.

Chapter 5

Christmas - B
Sir William & the Doll

Scripture: (Midnight Mass)

- Isaiah 9: 1-6
- Psalm 96: 1-2a, 2b-3, 11-12, 13
- Titus 2: 11-14
- Luke 2: 1-14

Today, Catholic Christians celebrate Christmas, the birth of the Christ Child.

On behalf of all the staff, faculty, and other ministers of our parish and its schools and ministries, I wish you and those you love a very Merry Christmas!

This day celebrates the story of Mary and Joseph going to the city of Bethlehem to register for a census ordered by the government. While they were there, Mary delivered a baby in a stable, for there was no room for them at an inn. Joseph and Mary named the child Jesus as had been commanded by the Angel Gabriel several months earlier. Following Jesus' birth, an angel appeared to shepherds who were watching over their flocks by night, telling them that he had good news of great joy for all people. After this announcement, a multitude of angels appeared, praising God saying: "Glory to God in the highest and on earth peace to those on whom his favor rests" (Luke 2: 14).

Christmas, in the United States, outshines all other holidays. Nothing is so magical as Christmas and its stories, music, and customs.

Christmas is a time to forget our bills and problems and worries. They will still be there when Christmas Eve and Christmas Day are history.

Christmas is also a time for remembering. We are called to remember Christmases of the past and our families and loved ones.

Finally, Christmas is a time to jolt us out of our little worlds and all of their tempest-in-a-teacup daily dramas. It is a time to remember what Christmas really means. It calls us to remember that the primary thing we are celebrating is not candy canes and flying reindeer, kisses under mistletoe and presents under the Christmas tree. Rather, the primary thing we celebrate on Christmas is the birth of our Savior. And when we try to grasp this concept, we are startled to discover this divine Savior – the King of the Universe – was born in a stable of a poor family.

Imagine that! The King of the Universe lying down with sheep and cows and who-knows-what-else! Just as today, the poor of Jesus' time were not treated with the same dignity and respect as the rich and powerful. Thus, it is easy to imagine that this might have been the lot of Jesus, Mary and Joseph.

But because God chose to have Jesus born in a manger, we have a very clear message: treat all people with dignity and respect, for all are children of God. All people, no matter how poor or forsaken or lowly, are our brothers and sisters. This, I think, is one of the greatest lessons of the Christmas story. This realization should lead us to treat everyone as though they are important in this world, for indeed they are.

In the following story, we hear about a very famous physician who showed the rest of us how vitally important it is to make all people feel important, because indeed, as children of God, they are. The physician was Sir William Osler, a Canadian who lived from 1849-1919.

One day, Sir William decided to visit the children's ward of a London hospital. He was delighted to see all of the children playing at one end of a large ward. But then he noticed one small girl who sat off to the side by herself, alone on her bed, a doll in her arms. Sir William could easily see that the little girl was feeling very lonely.

Sir William asked the head nurse about the little girl. The nurse told him that the other children ostracized the child. The mother of the little girl was dead, and her father had come to visit her only one time. It was at that one visit that the father had brought his little girl the doll that she clutched so tightly. Apart from that, no one had ever come to visit the little girl. Because of that, the other children of the ward had concluded that she was unimportant and had treated her with disdain.

Fortunately, Sir William was at his very best at moments like that, so he immediately came over to the little girl's bed. He said in a voice loud enough that the other children who were playing could hear, "May I sit down, please? I can't stay long on this visit, but I have wanted to see you badly." The head nurse, and others who were observing Sir William's visit, all said the little girl's eyes became electric with joy.

For several minutes, the physician talked with the little girl in a quiet, almost secretive tone. He asked the little girl about her doll's health, and he took out his stethoscope and carefully listened to the doll's heart.

When he was done with that, he said in a voice loud enough for the other children to hear, "You won't forget our secret, will you? And mind you, don't tell anyone." As Sir William Osler left the room, he turned to see the once ignored little girl suddenly become the center of attention of every other child in the ward.

This is a beautiful story to hear at Christmas time, for it reminds us that one of the most precious things people desire is to feel important.

After all, this is part of Jesus' triple love commandment – to love God, to love our neighbor, as we love our self. And there is no other way to show love of our neighbors than to treat them with dignity and respect, for like the little girl in the story, and like the Christ Child, every human being is, indeed, SOMEBODY.

And that is the good news I have for you on this Christmas.

Story source: Gordon MacDonald, "The Doctor," in William J. Bausch, *A World of Stories for Preachers and Teachers*, Mystic, Connecticut: Twenty-Third Publications, 1998, #100, pp. 248-249.

Chapter 6

Holy Family - B
Love Produces Miracles

Scripture:

- Genesis 15: 1-6; 21: 1-3
- Psalm 105: 1-2, 3-4, 6-7, 8-9
- Hebrews 11: 8, 11-12, 17-19
- Luke 2: 22-40

Today, Catholic Christians celebrate the Feast of the Holy Family of Jesus, Mary and Joseph. When I was a student in a Catholic school as a child, the concept of the Holy Family was so important that before we wrote any paper, we wrote "J.M.J." in the corner of the page to remind us of Jesus, Mary, and Joseph. We were encouraged to look at this family as an ideal.

But the feast of the Holy Family also reminds each of us to reflect on our own families. "Family" refers to whatever group of people you consider to be your family. These families may be biological, legal, or spiritual in nature. It doesn't matter how you define this term. What does matter is that all family members are called to nurture each other unconditionally, to continually challenge each other to grow and flourish, and to celebrate each other's achievements. This unconditional love is seen in the following story called "Love Produces Miracles."

There was once a baby boy born in a Milwaukee hospital. The baby was born not only blind, but he was mentally retarded and had cerebral palsy. He did not respond to sound or touch. His parents abandoned him.

The hospital staff did not know what to do with the child. Then, someone mentioned May Lemke, a nurse who lived near the hospital. May had already raised five children of her own, and she was known to be a very caring and competent person. The hospital staff asked May if she would raise the child. They assured her that "He will probably die young."

May responded to the request by saying, "I'll be happy to take the baby, but he won't die young."

May named the baby Les. It wasn't easy to care for him because he had so many needs. Every day, she massaged Les' body, prayed over him, and cried over him. One of May's neighbors told May that she was wasting her life caring for a baby like Les.

Years passed – five, ten, fifteen. It wasn't until Les was sixteen years old that May was able to teach him to stand by himself. All this time, Les never responded to May. Nevertheless, May continued to love him and pray for him and care for him. Then one day, May noticed Les' finger plucking a string on a package. She wondered if it was possible that Les was sensitive to music.

May began to surround Les with music. She played every kind of music imaginable for Les, hoping that it might touch something inside him. Eventually, May and her husband bought a second-hand piano and put it in Les' room. May took Les' fingers and showed him how to push the keys down, but Les didn't appear to understand.

Then one winter night, May awoke to the sound of someone playing a melody from Tchaikovsky's *Piano Concerto No. 1*. May and her husband were astonished to discover Les sitting at the piano smiling and playing the piece by ear. Les had never gotten out of bed before, and he had never seated himself at the piano before. He had never even struck a key on his own before. Now, he was playing beautifully.

Soon, Les began to live at the piano. He played not only classical music, but also country, ragtime, gospel, and rock music. It was incredible. All of the music that May had played for him had been stored in Les' brain, and now it was flowing out through his hands into the piano.

When he was twenty-eight years old, Les began to talk. His conversations were very simple, but he did ask questions and was able to give simple answers and make brief statements.

The physicians described Les as an autistic savant, a person who is brain damaged, but extremely talented. Though scientists cannot explain this phenomenon, they have known about this interesting condition for a couple of centuries. An autistic savant, played by Dustin Hoffman, was portrayed in recent times in the movie "Rain Man."

May Lemke cannot explain how Les was able to play the music. She only knows that unconditional love, persevering through time, had something to do with Les' gaining a better quality of life.

This beautiful story illustrates a most remarkable outcome of unconditional love and perseverance. Certainly the love of May Lemke was something all of us would hold to be noble and worthy of modeling.

As we continue our life journeys this week, it would be a good idea to reflect on our own families. How do we show love? How do we challenge our family members to be all they can be? How do we shower our family members with praise in the accomplishments?

And that is the good news I have for you on this Feast of the Holy Family.

Story source: Anonymous, "Love Produces Miracles," in Brian Cavanaugh (Ed.), *Sower's Seeds of Engagement: Fifth Planting*, New York: Paulist Press, 1998, #45, pp. 39-40.

Chapter 7

Epiphany of the Lord - B
Artaban

Scripture:

- Isaiah 60: 1-6
- Psalm 72: 1-2, 7-8, 10-11, 12-13
- Ephesians 3: 2-3a, 5-6
- Matthew 2: 1-12

Today, Catholic Christians celebrate the Feast of the Epiphany of the Lord. In the western branch of the Catholic Church, of which we are part, this feast day celebrates the manifestation of Jesus to the wise men who followed a special star to find the Christ Child. This ancient feast is sometimes called Little Christmas or the Feast of the Three Kings.

In the Epiphany story, we hear of visitors from the East bringing Jesus three gifts: gold, frankincense, and myrrh. The gold represents the kingship of Jesus, the frankincense represents his divinity, and the myrrh represents his eventual death.

In some parts of the world, including right here in our own parish, the Three Magi bring presents to children on this day.

For us, this feast is important because the Epiphany shows that Jesus is for all people, not just the Jewish people. He is for us. And unlike the wise men who had to search far and wide to find him, we have already found Jesus. Unfortunately, we sometimes forget this. We think Jesus is confined to a tabernacle in the church when, in reality, he lives in all human beings. That is the message we hear about in the following story by Henry van Dyke called "The Story of the Other Wise Man."

Long ago, in the time of Jesus, four wise men heard that there was born in Bethlehem the long-awaited Messiah, the King of the Jews. Now, most people have heard about three of the wise men, whom people in the Middle Ages named Caspar, Melchior, and Balthazar. Most people, though, have never heard of the fourth wise man, Artaban. This is his story.

When the wise men heard about the birth of Jesus, they decided to search for the Christ Child and bring him gifts. Caspar, Melchior, and Balthazar gathered their gifts of gold, frankincense, and myrrh, and set off to find the child. Unfortunately, Artaban was very busy at the time, so he didn't get to go with the other wise men. However, he did buy a bag of precious jewels to give the Christ Child as a present.

After his three friends left to find the Child, Artaban lost track of them. In fact, he never did learn where they went, for they never returned.

Artaban searched for the Christ Child for many years. Often, on his journey, he would encounter dying beggars, frightened mothers, and a wide assortment of people who were having terrible problems on their journeys through life. Because he was not only a wise man, but also a very compassionate and loving man, Artaban would often sell one of the jewels to help those in need.

After searching for the Christ Child for about thirty-three years, Artaban returned to Jerusalem. The time was the Jewish feast of Passover. But this was not an ordinary Passover time in the city. Rather, there was commotion in the streets. People told Artaban that they were going to a place outside of the city called Golgotha to see two robbers and a man named Jesus of Nazareth executed on crosses. The people told Artaban that the government was going to kill Jesus because he claimed to be the Son of God and King of the Jews.

Instinctively, Artaban knew in his heart that this Jesus was the King he had been searching for. Therefore, he rushed to the scene. But on his way, he met a young girl who was being sold into slavery. When the girl saw Artaban's royal robes, she fell at his feet and pleaded with him to rescue her. His heart was moved with pity for the girl, so he took his last jewel out of the bag and ransomed her. Just then, darkness fell over the land, and the earth shook, and great stones fell into the streets. One of them fell on Artaban, crushing his head.

As he lay dying in the arms of the girl he had just ransomed, he cried out weakly, "Three and thirty years I have looked for you, Lord, but I have never seen your face nor ministered to you!" But then a voice came out of the heavens, strong and kind, and said, "Inasmuch as you did good for the least of my brothers and sisters, you did it to me." At these words, Artaban's face grew calm and peaceful. His long journey had ended, for he had found his King!

Like Artaban, we too have found Jesus every time we have treated other human beings with dignity and respect. We too have served Jesus every time we have given drink to the thirsty or food to the hungry. We too have served Jesus every time we have cared for the sick, consoled the sorrowful, and visited those in prison. We too have served Jesus every time we have educated the ignorant and buried the dead. And because we have recognized Jesus and served him as he requested, God will certainly reward us. He has promised us this in many parts of the New Testament. For example, in the Gospel of Matthew Jesus says, "And whoever gives only a cup of cold water to one of these little ones to drink because he is a disciple—amen, I say to you, he will surely not lose his reward" (Matthew 10: 42).

As we continue our life journeys this week, it would be a good idea to reflect on how we serve God by serving others. Do we always recognize Jesus in the least among us – the poor, the suffering, and the marginalized? Are we generous with our time and talent and treasure towards such people?

And that is the good news I have for you on this Feast of the Epiphany of the Lord.

Story source: Henry van Dyke, "Artaban," in William J. Bausch (Ed.), *A World of Stories for Preachers and Teachers*, Mystic, Connecticut: Twenty-Third Publications, 1998, #134, p. 281.

Chapter 8

Baptism of the Lord - B
Little Joe

Scripture:

- Isaiah 55: 1-11
- Isaiah 12: 2-3, 4bcd, 5-6
- 1 John 5: 1-9
- Mark 1: 7-11

Today, Catholic Christians celebrate the Feast of the Baptism of the Lord.

In the Gospel of Mark, we read a beautiful story of the Blessed Trinity in action. John the Baptist is baptizing Jesus, who is God the Son, in the river. As Jesus comes out of the water, God the Holy Spirit, appearing as a dove, descends on him. The voice of God the Father then says, "You are my beloved Son; with you I am well pleased" (Mark 1: 11).

The story should remind us of our own baptism when God the Father chose us to be followers of Jesus Christ and filled us with the Holy Spirit.

On this day, I share a beautiful baptism story by a nurse named Beverly Houseman.

Some years ago, Beverly Houseman attended a Catholic nursing school. Interestingly enough, no one in her class, including Beverly, was a Catholic. Rather, all of the nursing students were either Pentecostals or Baptists, and neither of these Protestant denominations believes in infant baptism.

Because of their beliefs, the students all said they would refuse to baptize a baby in the case of an emergency. Because of their refusal, Sr. James Cecilia told the group, "You knew this was a Catholic school when you applied. You should also have known that you would have to adhere to our teachings."

The twenty-four nursing students of the class decided to compromise. They promised. They agreed they would learn the procedure of baptism if they would never actually have to do it. With that compromise, they were able to advance in their nursing studies.

Years went by, and Beverly moved to Ohio with her husband Harley. Beverly got a job in a small eighty-bed hospital where many of the staff members were Catholic. Therefore, she never had to worry about baptizing any infants.

Then, one stormy night, Beverly was asked to baptize a baby. A woman had come into the hospital from the raging storm and gave birth two months prematurely to a baby that weighed only two pounds and one ounce. The nursing staff believed that the infant had little chance of surviving. Because this was a small hospital, the nursery was rather primitive. It had no neonatologists, only incubators, oxygen and prayer.

The staff did its best to keep the little boy alive. They knew they had to keep the incubator at 98 degrees F.

When Beverly went to see the mother, she said, "I want him baptized!" When Beverly phoned the priest, he told her that he had no transportation and would not be able to come until the next day. Beverly then called the nursing supervisor who was Catholic, but she had the day off. Amazingly enough, not a single Catholic staff member was on duty in the hospital that night.

Beverly went back to the infant's mother and explained that she was not Catholic and that her denomination did not believe in infant baptism. Beverly said that she would baptize the baby if the mother insisted on it, or they could just pray during the night and hope the infant be alive by morning when the priest came. Because the mother was adamant in her desire to have the child baptized, Beverly agreed.

Beverly took a sterile medicine cup, sterile water, and sterile cotton balls. She lifted the precious little head in the palm of her hand and, with the other hand, poured the water on his head saying, "Joseph Sánchez, I baptize you, conditionally, in the name of the Father, the Son, and the Holy Spirit." With tears running down her face, she handed Joseph to his mother.

Over the next months, the staff gave special care to Joseph, and he captured their hearts. In fact, the staff began calling him "Little Joe." Each day, the nurses would pray that Little Joe would live at least until their shift was over.

Then, one afternoon, when Beverly came to work, the outgoing staff said, "Little Joe had a bad day, and he may not live through the night." Beverly prayed, "Please, Lord, don't take him on my watch."

After making rounds on all the other babies, Beverly came back to Little Joe. The temperature gauge of the incubator read 80 degrees F instead of the 98 degrees F it was supposed to be. She discovered the electrical plug lying on the floor. After plugging it back in, she called her pastor and others to pray for Little Joe. He lived through the night.

Beverly was then off-duty for three days. When she returned to work, she discovered that Little Joe, having reached 5 pounds, had been discharged. She was very sad, for she had not said good-bye to the little miracle baby.

The years went by. Then, one night, Beverly's husband Harley came back from a men's church dinner. "Wait until you see what I have for you!" In his hand was a picture of a teenager. On the back was this message:

Dear Mrs. Houseman:

My name is Joseph Sánchez. I am fourteen years old and weigh 140 pounds. Thank you for taking care of me when I was born.

Little Joe

As we continue our life journeys this week, it would be a good idea to reflect on our own baptisms. How do we reflect the Holy Spirit who lives in us? How do we show the world, by our actions, that we are Christians? Do we even know the date of our spiritual birthday, the day we were baptized?

And that is the good news I have for you on this Feast of the Baptism of the Lord.

Story source: Beverly Houseman, "I Baptize You…" in Jack Canfield, Mark Victor Hansen, Nancy Mitchell-Autio, and LeAnn Thieman (Eds.), *Chicken Soup for the Nurse's Soul*, 2001, pp. 99-102.

Part Two

LENT &
EASTER SEASONS

Chapter 9

1st Sunday of Lent - B
The Nose of the Camel

Scripture:

- Genesis 9: 8-15
- Psalm 25 4-5ab, 6 & 7bc, 8-9
- 1 Peter 3: 18-22
- Mark 1: 12-15

Today, Catholic Christians celebrate the First Sunday of Lent.

On this day, we hear the famous story of Jesus living in the desert for forty days. During this time, he was tempted by the devil.

Temptation, in the way I'm using it in this homily, refers to a desire to act in a way that we may enjoy in the short term, but which we will probably regret later. Tempting others means enticing them to engage in some action that is pleasing in the short term, but will probably have negative consequences later.

Stories about temptation are always relevant, because every one of us is tempted every day to do things we know we should not do. Sometimes we are like Jesus, who resisted temptation, but sometimes we give in. When we give in, we generally make things worse for our lives. That is what we see in the following story that I'll call "The nose of the camel."

There was once an Arab who was riding his camel across the desert. As they traveled, the wind began to get stronger and stronger. The Arab knew that soon the wind would be so bad that blowing sand would completely block their view.

Therefore, the Arab stopped and quickly put up his little tent. After the tent was set up, the Arab got inside where it was calm and safe from the storm outside. Soon, the howling desert wind lulled him to sleep.

After he had been asleep only a short while, he heard a noise from his camel. His camel, named Fatima, had stuck her nose under the flap of the tent. Fatima said, "Master, the wind is very strong outside, and it is getting very cold. Is it okay if I let my nose stay inside your tent?"

The Arab said, "Certainly. There is certainly enough room in this little tent for your nose to keep warm." After saying that, the Arab went back to sleep.

Soon, however, Fatima said, "Master, would it be okay if I just let my front legs come into the tent? It is getting colder and colder outside."

"Certainly," replied the Arab. The Arab then scooted over a bit, for the tent was quite small.

Soon afterwards, however, the camel woke up the Arab again and said, "I hate to bother you again, but the desert night is absolutely freezing. May I bring my whole self into the tent?"

The Arab replied, "Okay, Fatima. Come into the tent completely." So, Fatima moved herself into the tent. Together, the Arab and Fatima hardly

THE NOSE OF THE CAMEL

fit. Soon, the Arab was sound asleep. When he woke up, however, he was amazed to find himself not inside the tent, but rather, outside in the cold. The camel, meanwhile, was a snug as she could be, having the whole tent for herself.

Nobody knows exactly the origin of this story, but it certainly is a good one, for it gives us a vivid image of how powerful temptation can be. Here are just three things we can learn about the concept of temptation.

First, I think most people would agree that it is easier to prevent temptation than to confront it. We hear the same principle in terms of health and illness: "An ounce of prevention is worth a pound of cure," and we daily pray "lead us not into temptation."

Many people, for example, play head games, deliberately flirting with trouble. People on weight-loss diets, for example, do this all the time. They might go to the grocery store and instead of buying a little pie that has 330 calories, they buy a regular-size pie with more than 1,900 calories. They rationalize this purchase by saying, "Well, I'll just have one piece." That is like the person who buys a huge bag of potato chips saying they will eat only "one serving – 4 chips." No way is that going to happen, for once we give in to pure pleasure, it is very difficult to stop! It is much easier to avoid buying the pie or chips to begin with, or simply to buy a small package to kill the craving.

Second, all of us face temptations every day. Our lives are filled to the brim with things we would like to do wrong. And when I say this, I'm not talking about "biggies" such as robbing a bank or killing people. Rather, I'm talking about telling someone off who has been aggravating us, or engaging in delicious gossip, so delicious that we think we would burst if we didn't tell someone.

Because we find temptations all around us every day, we should not go looking for new temptations to battle. Jesus told us that very thing when he said, "Do not worry about tomorrow; tomorrow will take care of itself. Sufficient for a day is its own evil" (Matthew 6: 34). In other words, don't go looking for trouble.

And third, don't get discouraged when you fail to overcome a temptation. We all fail from time to time. Rather than becoming discouraged, pick yourself up and move on. Just as God is always willing to forgive us, we need to mimic him and learn to forgive ourselves. If we don't learn how to do this, we will be miserable for the rest of our lives, and that will affect our spiritual, mental, and physical health. Thus, forgiveness is a pro-life issue.

As we continue our life journeys this week, it would be a good idea to reflect on the temptations we face every day. How do we try to avoid them? How do we sometimes fail? How do we forgive ourselves as God does?

And that is the good news I have for you on this First Sunday of Lent.

Story source: Various forms of the story of the camel's nose inside the tent may be found on www.CamelStories.com.

Chapter 10

2nd Sunday of Lent - B
Brother Van of Montana

Scripture:

- Genesis 22: 1-2, 9a, 10-13, 15-18
- Psalm 116: 10 & 15, 16-17, 18-19
- Romans 8: 31b-34
- Mark 9: 2-10

Today, Catholic Christians celebrate the Second Sunday of Lent.

On this day, we hear a rhetorical question that St. Paul put to the Romans, a query that we repeat even today, two thousand years later: "Brothers and sisters: if God is for us, who can be against us?" (Romans 8: 31b).

And in the Gospel reading from St. Mark, we hear the Transfiguration story. In this story, Jesus is with Peter, James, and John on a mountain. Suddenly, Jesus' clothes became dazzling white, and Moses and Elijah appeared with him. Both Moses and Elijah, remember, had been long dead at the time Jesus walked the earth.

The apostles were both amazed and terrified, and they wanted to show honor to Jesus, Moses, and Elijah by building a tent for each. Suddenly, however, a voice came from the heavens saying, "This is my beloved Son. Listen to him" (Mark 9: 7b).

This story is important to us because it reminds us that Jesus, alone, is the one we are to follow. The voice in the story is God the Father, and the Son is Jesus. Both Moses, who represents the Old Testament laws, and Elijah, who represents the Old Testament prophets, disappear in the story, leaving just Jesus. The moral is that much of the law and prophets of the Old Testament are things of the past. Now we are to follow the fulfillment of the Old Testament, which is Jesus.

Through the ages, there have always been people who have not only recognized Jesus as the star to follow, but also proclaimed this message to others. One such person was a preacher named William Wesley Van Orsdel.

Willie, as he was called as a youth, was born near Gettysburg, Pennsylvania on March 20, 1848. Because his parents died before he was 13 years old, William's aunt raised him and his brothers and sisters on a farm near Gettysburg.

When he was 15 years old, Willie had a conversion experience at the little Methodist prayer meeting his family attended. For the rest of his teenage years, Willie kept having powerful visions. These visions involved preaching to cowboys, miners, stagecoach drivers, freighters, and Indians.

Like others who receive the call to preach, Willie knew that he could not find peace in his spirit if he did not answer the call. Therefore, at the age of 24, Willie gave up farming, said farewell to Pennsylvania, grabbed his Bible, and headed for Montana. He traveled to Sioux City, Iowa where he was able to catch a Missouri River steamboat traveling to Fort Benton, Montana. Willie was the only passenger on this cargo vessel, and the captain let him ride at half price. All he had to do was help the crew gather wood and do some preaching and singing along the way.

Willie arrived in Fort Benton, Montana on Sunday, July 1, 1872. He planned on being a Methodist circuit-riding preacher on horseback to the Blackfoot Indian tribe. One day, as he was going to the Blackfoot reservation, he decided to preach in a saloon named the Four Deuces. When he introduced himself to the people in the saloon as William Wesley Van Orsdel, the people decided that name was too long and too formal for Montana. Therefore, they told him that from then on, his name would be Brother Van.

At first, the cowboys didn't want to have anything to do with him. After all, they came to the saloon to drink and have a good time, not to listen to a preacher. Fortunately, though, the saloonkeeper told the crowd that Brother Van would preach that day, and if they didn't like it, they could leave. The saloonkeeper noted that every one of them was a sinner; so a little preaching couldn't possibly hurt them.

Brother Van began to sing, and the piano player, with a cigar in his mouth, began to play along. After singing the hymn, Brother Van began to preach. The men, however, begged him to keep singing, for they had not heard anyone sing in a long time. So, only after he sang the song three times was Brother Van permitted to preach.

Brother Van not only preached that day in the Four Deuces Saloon, he preached all over the State of Montana. In fact, he spent the next 47 years of his life preaching to Indians, miners, farmers, alcoholics, brothel keepers, saloon owners, cowboys, and anyone who would listen. People far and wide grew to love and respect Brother Van, for they knew he cared for them and never looked down on them. In fact, he became so famous that people could simply write "Brother Van Montana" on an envelope and it would be delivered to him.

Even though people far and wide came to love him, sometimes people who did not yet know him would give him trouble. For example, he was once mistaken for a horse thief and almost hanged, but God protected him from harm.

From 1892 to 1918, as superintendent of the Methodists' North Montana Mission, Brother Van built 100 churches, 50 parsonages, six hospitals, a school for orphans, and Montana Wesleyan College. Brother Van, who remained single all his life, died in 1919. He was inducted into the Montana Cowboy Hall of Fame in 2011.

It is always inspirational for us to read of people who live the Transfiguration story, continually keeping their eyes on Jesus and only Jesus. From such people, we can learn much.

And that is the good news I have for you on this Second Sunday of Lent.

Story source: "William Van Orsdel – Brother Van –(1848-1919). Montana Cowboy Hall of Fame, 2011.

"Montana's Evangelist-at-Large: Brother Van (William Wesley Van Orsdel – 1848-1919," www.ChristianHistory.Net, April 1, 2000.

Chapter 11

3rd Sunday of Lent - B
Tibetan Happiness

Scripture:

- Exodus 20: 1-17
- Psalm 19: 8, 9, 10, 11
- 1 Corinthians 1: 22-25
- John 2: 13-25

Today, Catholic Christians celebrate the Third Sunday of Lent.

On this day, we read about some of the commandments of the Old Testament. These rules, sometimes called the Ten Commandments, are found in the Book of Exodus.

Many Catholic Christians use this group of rules to do their "examination of conscience" before celebrating the Sacrament of Reconciliation. They do this for two reasons. First, these ten rules are all in one place, so they are easy to identify. Second, they do this because following these Old Testament commandments is so much easier than to follow the New Testament's Christian commandments. The Christian commandments include such things as: forgive your enemy; pray for those who hurt you; welcome the stranger; do to others what you would have them do to you; do not store up treasures on earth; stop judging; and many more.

And whatever the commandments, be they Jewish or Christian, we sometimes do not truly grasp their meaning. We attempt to follow them by acting in a certain way without understanding their purpose and/or without changing our inner disposition.

Let's look at just one of the Old Testament rules about not coveting one's neighbor's things, and how one young man failed miserably to truly live in harmony with this Jewish law.

There was once a young man I'll call Tony. Tony was a bright premed student at Harvard University, one of the most prestigious universities in the United States. The summer after his sophomore year, he went on vacation to the mountains of Tibet. There, he met a monk who said to him, "Don't you see how you are poisoning your soul with your success-oriented way of life? You stay up all night studying for exams so that you can get better grades than your friends. Your idea of a happy marriage is not finding a wonderful woman who will make you whole, but rather, finding a woman that all the other men want. That is not how people are supposed to live. A life filled with competition is not fulfilling. Give it up. Come and join my fellow monks and me. Live as we live, loving each other and living in harmony. Here you can find true happiness."

Tony heard these words at a very impressionable time in his life. He had just finished four years in a very competitive high school to get into Harvard, and he had worked very hard to become one of the top premed students in his class at the university. The idea, then, of becoming a Tibetan monk was very appealing. Just imagine – living life without competition!

After thinking it over, Tony made a decision. He called his parents and told them he would not be coming home. He was dropping out of Harvard to live in a Buddhist monastery in Tibet.

Six months later, he wrote to his parents: "Dear Mom and Dad, I know that you were not happy with the decision I made last summer to join the monastery. But I want you to know that I have never been happier. For the first time in my life, I am at peace. Here, there is no competing, no hustling, and no trying to get ahead of anyone else. Here, we are all equal, and we all share everything we have with each other. This way of life is so much in harmony with the inner essence of my soul, that in only six months I have become the #2 disciple in the entire community. I'm delighted to say that by June, I think I can become number one!"

In this story, poor Tony tried to change his life. Unfortunately, however, he only changed the location of his body. He did not change his heart. His competitive nature, a telltale symptom of pride, was left intact.

We can always learn, however, from any story. Here are just three things we can learn from Scripture passages involving rules and from Tony's story.

First, we need to be careful not to engage in ritualism. Ritualism is falling in love with rules, including laws, without understanding the purpose for which they were created in the first place. In our country, for example, Catholic Christians are asked to abstain from meat on Ash Wednesday. The purpose of this rule is to help us make a sacrifice showing that the spirit is stronger than the body. Some people, however, are ritualists; they observe the "letter" of the law but ignore the "spirit" of the law. On Ash Wednesday, for example, they might spend $75 on a lobster tail dinner with a bottle of champagne and "give up" eating a $1.00 hamburger, all the while patting themselves on the back for being such good Catholics.

Second, and related to the first point, is that we need to change our hearts to be in harmony with God. Some people go around "acting holy," but inside, they are less than holy. Jesus called such people "whited sepulchers" or "whitened tombs." He called such people "hypocrites" who

"...appear beautiful on the outside, but inside are full of dead men's bones and every kind of filth. Even so, on the outside you appear righteous, but inside you are filled with hypocrisy and evildoing" (Matthew 23: 27-28).

And third, although we are required to keep Old Testament rules such as the "ten commandments," as Christians we need to keep the Christian commandments, those found in the New Testament.

As we continue our life journey this week, it would be a good idea to reflect on our own faith journey. Are our hearts in harmony with our good actions? Are we just as eager to follow the Christian commandments, as we are to follow the Old Testament's Jewish commandments?

And that is the good news I have for you on this Third Sunday of Lent.

Story source: Anonymous, "Finding Happiness in Tibet," in Wayne Rice (Editor), *Still More Hot Illustrations for Youth Talks*, Grand Rapids, Michigan: Zondervan/Youth Specialties, 1999, pp. 61-62.

Chapter 12

4th Sunday of Lent - B
The Art Auction

Scripture:

- 2 Chronicles 36: 14-16, 19-23
- Psalm 137: 1-2, 3, 4-5, 6
- Ephesians 2: 4-10
- John 3: 14-21

Today, Catholic Christians celebrate the Fourth Sunday of Lent.

On this day, we hear in St. Paul's letter to the Ephesians that we have been saved by God's great love for us. Paul reminds us, however, that we should not go around boasting about this, for we did nothing to deserve it. Our salvation is a gift, pure and simple. Specifically, Paul says, "For by grace you have been saved through faith, and this is not from you; it is the gift of God; it is not from works, so no one may boast" (Ephesians 2: 8-9).

Sometimes we need to be reminded that our salvation does not depend on us. It depends on God's gift to us through Jesus. For if we forget that God the Son is our savior, we begin to create a false idol – our self – and begin to imagine that we are capable of "earning" this gift. That is what we see in the following story by Joel Lusz called "The Art Auction."

There was once an elderly widowed man who had just one child, a son named Mark. The elderly man was justifiably proud because Mark had become a very talented art collector. Mark had a trained eye and a sharp business mind. The father beamed with pride as he and Mark dealt with art collectors from around the world.

One winter, however, Mark was forced to leave the comfort of his home to go to war. After just a few short weeks, Mark's father received a telegram saying that his beloved son had been killed while saving the life of a fellow soldier. The father, who had always loved Christmas, now had to face the upcoming Christmas season alone and sad.

On Christmas morning, a knock at the front door awoke the old man. When he got to the door, he discovered a soldier standing there with a package under his arm. After being invited in and seated, the soldier began to talk.

He told the father how he had been a close friend of Mark and how Mark had rescued dozens of wounded soldiers before a bullet stilled his caring heart. As the father listened to the story of bravery of his son, the pride he felt for his son began to ease his grief.

Then the soldier placed the package on the father's lap and said, "I'm an artist. I want you to have this."

When the old man unwrapped the present, he found a portrait of his son that the soldier had painted. The image was a work of genius, perfectly capturing his son's face.

After the young soldier had left, Mark's father placed the portrait over the fireplace as his most precious possession. To do so, he had to move a painting worth tens of thousands of dollars. During the weeks that followed, the old man grew peaceful. He told his neighbors and friends that the portrait was the greatest gift he had ever received.

The following spring, the old man grew ill and died. The entire art world stirred in anticipation of the public auction that would take place. They knew that the old man's home was filled with amazing paintings from all over the world. They also knew that the collection was worth millions of dollars.

In his will, the old man had stipulated that the auction must be public and held on Christmas day, for that was the day when he had received his most precious gift.

On the big day of the auction, the auctioneer began with the portrait of the son. Someone from the back of the room said, "Who cares about that painting? It's worthless. Let's get to the real treasures." The auctioneer replied, "No, we must start with this painting of the old man's son."

Though the auctioneer tried to start the bidding for the portrait of Mark at $100, nobody would bid on it. Finally, a friend of the old man said, "Sir, I would love to have that painting. I only have ten dollars, though." Nobody else bid anything, so the auctioneer lowered the gavel indicating that the portrait was now the possession of the deceased man's friend, for just ten dollars.

The auctioneer then said, to the astonishment of everyone, "Thank you for coming everyone. The auction is now over." The crowd was stunned. People began to shout, shouting that there were millions of dollars worth of paintings, and they wanted to bid on them. They didn't come to get a picture of some old guy's son!

The auctioneer replied, "It is very simple. According to the will of the father, whoever takes the son, gets it all."

This was a huge surprise for all of the people in this story, but it should not be a surprise for us as Christians. As Christians, we have been assured of salvation. God has given us the gift of our faith, and we have graciously accepted it. We treasure this gift. We have taken the Son, and as a result, we "get it all." What amazing, stunning, and joyful news this is.

As we continue our life journeys this week, it would be a good idea to reflect on the gift of our faith. Do we thank God for our Catholic Christian faith every day? Or do we just take it for granted?

And that is the good news I have for you on this Fourth Sunday of Lent.

Story source: "The Art Auction" by Joel Lusz. In Wayne Rice (Editor), *Still More Hot Illustrations for Youth Talks*, Grand Rapids, Michigan: Zondervan/Youth Specialties, 1999, pp. 120-122.

Chapter 13

5th Sunday of Lent - B
Fr. Rutilio Grande

Scripture:
_____

- Jeremiah 31: 31-34
- Psalm 51: 3-4, 12-13, 14-15
- Hebrews 5: 7-9
- John 12: 20-33

Today, Catholic Christians celebrate the Fifth Sunday of Lent.

On this day, we hear Jesus say to his disciples, "Amen, amen, I say to you, unless a grain of wheat falls to the ground and dies, it remains just a grain of wheat; but if it dies, it produces much fruit" (John 12: 24).

For over 2,000 years, the Catholic Church has held this teaching of Jesus to be very precious. We see how the Church treasures this teaching when it talks about the awesome nature of martyrdom, the giving of one's life for the Faith. In the early Church, for example, only martyrs were venerated as saints. Only later did the Church recognize that others could live lives worthy of being venerated as saints.

Today, we look at the life of one man who gave his life for the Faith and, as a result, is being considered for sainthood. His name was Rutilio Grande.

Rutilio was born on July 5, 1928 in El Paisnal, El Salvador. As a young man, he studied to become a priest at the seminary of San José de la Montaña in San Salvador, the capital city of El Salvador. While he was at the seminary, he became friends with another young man named Óscar Romero who would one day become the Archbishop of San Salvador.

Rutilio was ordained a priest in 1959. He then went to Spain to study, and in 1965, returned to El Salvador. From 1965 to 1970, he worked in the seminary as the director of social action projects, and he was also a professor of pastoral theology there. In 1975, he was the master of ceremonies at the installation of his friend, Óscar Romero, as the bishop of the diocese of Santiago de María.

In 1972, Fr. Rutilio Grande began working in the parish of Aguilares. With fellow Jesuits, he began to establish Christian base communities and teaching *Delegados de la Palabra* (Delegates of the Word) to lead these small communities. To fully understand the need for small Christian base communities and the need to train lay leaders for them, we must remember that in Latin American countries, parishes can have over 100,000 parishioners scattered over a large geographical area with many churches and chapels. Without *Delegados de la Palabra*, the people would have no Catholic presence except on those rare occasions when a priest could come for Mass.

We also must remember that by contrast with the United States where the majority of the people are middle class, the majority of the people in many nations of Latin America are poor. Fr. Rutilio knew this very well, and he had a passion for helping the poor. He often spoke against the injustices the poor suffered from the government and from rich landowners, and he spent much time helping organize marginalized rural farmers in El Salvador. Needless to say, local landowners saw him and his work as very dangerous, for they had no intention of helping poor peasants obtain their rights.

As Rutilio continued his work, other priests were being kidnapped and expelled from the country for championing the poor peasants.

On Saturday, March 12, 1977, Fr. Rutilio Grande was traveling through the sugar cane fields in the Aguilares parish on his way to evening Mass. Accompanying him in the truck were 72-year old Manual Solórzano and 16-year old Nelson Rutilio Lemus. Suddenly, machine gun fire killed all three of them.

When Óscar Romero, who was by then the Archbishop of San Salvador, learned of this tragedy, he immediately came to the church in Aguilares where the bodies of the two men and one teenager were laid. He listened to stories about how the local farmers suffered and how his friend, Fr. Rutilio Grande, had tried to help make their lives better.

Archbishop Romero was touched to the core of his being. The next morning, he announced that from that point on, he would not meet with any government official or attend any national event until Fr. Grande's death was investigated. He also cancelled all Masses throughout the archdiocese on a particular Sunday, saying he would celebrate just one Mass at the cathedral. 150 priests joined him for that Mass, and over 100,000 people attended.

On March 24, 1980, Archbishop Óscar Romero was shot to death while celebrating Mass in a little chapel near the cathedral. Today he, like his friend Fr. Rutilio Grande, is being considered for sainthood.

Although there are many things we can learn from the lives of Óscar and Rutilio, one of the things I find so interesting is that because of the killing of Fr. Rutilio, Archbishop Óscar Romero had a profound conversion experience. He said, "When I looked at Rutilio lying there dead I thought 'if they have killed him for doing what he did, then I too have to walk the same path.'" As a result of Rutilio's death, Óscar Romero took up the cause of the poor, becoming their champion in his preaching and other actions. And as a result, he lost his life. Indeed, what Jesus said was true: if a grain of wheat dies, it produces much fruit.

As we continue our life journeys this week, it would be a good idea to reflect on those in our Church who are putting the lives on the line in mission lands for the poor and the oppressed.

And that is the good news I have for you on this Fifth Sunday of Lent.

Story sources:

http://folingjesus.org/companions/romero.html

Thomas M. Kelly, "Challenging the Status Quo: Rutilio Grande, S.J. and the Poor," *Journal of Religion and Society*, Supplement 10 (2014)

Chapter 14

Palm Sunday of the Passion of the Lord – B
Holy Week

Scripture:

- Isaiah 50: 4-7
- Psalm 22: 8-9, 17-18a, 19-20, 23-24
- Philippians 2: 6-11
- Mark 14: 1 – 15: 47

On this Palm Sunday of the Lord's Passion, we begin the most special week of the year for Christians - Holy Week.

On this day, we read about the great welcome the people of Jerusalem gave to Jesus as he rode through the city. Then, however, we read the account of Jesus' passion, death and burial in the Gospel of Mark.

During Holy Week, the diocese will celebrate the Chrism Mass at St. Michael the Archangel parish in Cary, N.C. At that Mass, the bishop and priests will renew their priestly promises, and they will bless the three oils that will go to each parish for the coming year. The oils will be used to celebrate various sacraments in the parishes.

On the evening of Holy Thursday, we will begin a special Mass called the Mass of the Lord's Supper. As the Mass begins, the Season of Lent officially ends for Catholic Christians, and we enter a three-day Season called Triduum. At this Mass, the people will bring the three oils blessed at the Chrism Mass to the priest, and the priest will wash the feet of some people just as Jesus washed the feet of his apostles. The washing of the feet symbolizes the new form of leadership Jesus gave to his disciples; that is, to be the leader, one must be the servant of all. We call this the servant-leader model.

On Good Friday, we commemorate Jesus' Passion and Death. At the Basilica Shrine of St. Mary, we will have the traditional Catholic service that is in three parts: Reading of the Passion; Veneration of the Cross; and a Communion Service. The 2 p.m. service will be in English, and the 7 p.m. service will be in Spanish. The Hispanic community will have their annual "*Vía Crucis*" or "Way of the Cross" at 4 p.m. on Good Friday. Included in this pageant will be the enactment of the Fifteenth Station: the Resurrection of Jesus from the dead.

On Holy Saturday, we will celebrate the one Mass that is permitted that day at 8:00 p.m. The Mass is in both English and Spanish, and at this celebration we will have the Blessing of the New Fire, Blessing of the New Water, Blessing of the Easter Candle, and most importantly, we will celebrate Sacraments of Initiation (Baptism, Confirmation, and First Communion) for many of the people in our RCIA Ministry.

On Easter Sunday, we will have our regular Sunday Masses plus a 6:30 a.m. Mass in English. This year, we will also have extra Masses in the cafeteria at 9:30 a.m. and 11:00 a.m.

I hope you can make many of these celebrations.

And that is the good news I have for you on this Palm Sunday.

Chapter 15

Easter - B
Come Home

Scripture:

- Acts 10: 34a, 37-43
- Psalm 118: 1-2, 16-17, 22-23
- 1 Corinthians 5: 6b-8
- John 20: 1-9

Today, Catholic Christians celebrate the Resurrection of Jesus from the dead – Easter - the greatest feast day of the Catholic Church.

On this day, we hear St. Paul tell the Corinthians to "Clear out the old yeast, so that you may become a fresh batch of dough, inasmuch as you are unleavened. For our paschal lamb, Christ, has been sacrificed. Therefore, let us celebrate the feast, not with the old yeast, the yeast of malice and wickedness, but with the unleavened bread of sincerity and truth" (1 Corinthians 5: 7-8).

Paul's message is a resurrection message: we should rise from the old into the new, from the evil into the good, from the darkness into the light. Every day, as Christians, we are called to resurrection, to continually change and become more and more like Christ.

In his book called *No Wonder They Call Him Savior*, Max Lucado tells the story of how a young woman experienced a genuine resurrection experience thanks to the prayers and persistence of her loving mother.

There was once a mother named Maria who lived with her daughter Christina in a one-room, dirt floor house on a dusty street in a very poor neighborhood on the outskirts of a Brazilian village. Though it was poor, Maria and Christina tried to make the little house comfortable. They decorated it with a wooden crucifix, an old calendar, and the faded photo of a relative. The furnishings consisted of a wood-burning stove, a washbasin, and a pallet on either side of the room for sleeping.

Maria's husband had died when Christina was just an infant. The young mother refused every opportunity to get married again, got a job, and did her best to raise Christina by herself. The job she had as a maid provided sufficient food and clothes for Christina and herself. Finally, one day, Christina was old enough to get a job to help out with finances for the two of them.

Like her mother, Christina was a strong, independent-minded person. Though she was young and very beautiful, and though she could charm any young man with her sparkling personality, she rejected all attempts of young men to date her. She had her sights on something much bigger than the dusty little town where she lived.

Christina was filled with dreams of one day living in a big city with exciting avenues and city life. Maria, however, was horrified at the thought. She reminded Christina that city streets were very harsh, and there were no jobs for a young woman. What Maria was really worried about was that Christina would be forced to make money in ways contrary to her Christian faith. After all, Maria reasoned, when pride meets hunger, human beings will do things that they never thought they would do.

Then, one morning, Maria found Christina's bed empty. Immediately she knew that her daughter had left for the big city. She knew Maria had no way of earning money decently, and she knew her that Christina was too proud to admit defeat. Therefore, Maria went to a photograph booth in a variety store and took as many photos of herself as possible. Then, she took a bus to Rio de Janeiro.

In the city, Maria went to bars, hotels, nightclubs, and any other place where streetwalkers and prostitutes might be found. In every place, she left her picture taped the bulletin board or fastened to a phone booth. On the back of every photo of herself, Maria wrote a note.

Before long, however, Maria's money and photos ran out, and she had to return home. The weary, heartbroken mother wept as the bus began the long journey back to her little village.

It was a few weeks later that young Christina came down the stairs of the hotel where she was working. Her eyes no longer sparkled with joy and hope. On the contrary, they showed pain and fear. She no longer laughed. The dreams she once held about living in an exciting city had vanished. A thousand times over she wished she could trade the fancy beds she now knew for her simple, but secure, pallet in her mother's home.

When she reached the bottom of the stairs, she noticed a familiar face. She looked again, and there on the lobby mirror was a small photo of her mother. Christina's eyes burned, and her throat tightened as she walked across the room to remove the photo. Written on the back was this invitation: "Whatever you have done, whatever you have become, it doesn't matter. Please come home."

She did.

What a beautiful story this is for Easter, the time of resurrection not only for Jesus, but for all of us. It does not matter how far we stray away from the Lord, for he is always calling us to return, to become reborn in the Spirit.

Perhaps you have been away from the church for a long time, and God has led you here today. Welcome home! The past is gone. What we now have is a blank piece of paper, paper to write exciting new chapters in our lives. Make the most of it. And always remember that no matter where you have been, or what you have become, God loves you and always will.

As we continue our life journeys this Easter week, let's take a few minutes to reflect on our own resurrection experience. What do we need to leave behind, and how will we replace the old with the new?

And that is the good news I have for you this Easter Sunday.

Story source: Max Lucado, "Come Home," in Wayne Rice (Ed.), *Still More Hot Illustrations for Youth Talks*, Grand Rapids, Michigan: Zondervan/Youth Specialties, 1999, pp. 125-126.

Chapter 16

2nd Sunday of Easter - B
The Old Fisherman

Scripture:

- Acts 4: 32-35
- Psalm 118: 2-4, 13-15, 22-24
- 1 John 5: 1-6
- John 20: 19-31

Today, Catholic Christians celebrate the Second Sunday of Easter, sometimes called Divine Mercy Sunday.

On this day, we hear about how the early members of the Church shared all their possessions in common. Nobody was in need, because everyone received what he or she needed. After selling their houses, the people would give the money to the apostles who would then determine who needed what.

Today, there are very few Christian communities that live like the early Christians. Among those that do are some Catholic religious orders and a few Protestant denominations and sects.

Even though the majority of us do not live a Christian socialist way of life, we are all called to show mercy towards those in need. For some people, mercy means forgiving others when they have done something wrong. Although that is one definition of mercy, for Catholic Christians, mercy is much greater. Mercy, in Catholic theology, means showing love toward others, especially those who are in need. Though mercy originates from compassion or feeling sorry for someone in trouble, mercy happens by putting that compassion into action.

Catholic Christians often talk about two types of mercy: corporal and spiritual. The corporal works of mercy are focused on helping others with physical needs. They include feeding the hungry, giving drink to the thirsty, clothing the naked, visiting the sick, sheltering the homeless, visiting those in prison, and burying the dead. The spiritual works of mercy include instructing the ignorant, counseling the doubtful, admonishing sinners, bearing wrong patiently, forgiving others, comforting the afflicted, and praying for the living and the dead.

In the following story, we hear how one family showed mercy toward a stranger who showed up at their door one day. And as a result, they made friends with someone in need. The story comes from Fr. Tommy Lane's collection of stories.

There was once a family who lived across from John Hopkins Hospital in Baltimore. The family, composed of a mother, father, and their children, lived downstairs, and they rented the upstairs rooms for clinic patients.

One summer evening, while the wife was cooking supper, there was a knock at the door. When she opened the door, there stood a shriveled-up man with a lopsided face that was swollen, red and raw.

"I've come to see if I can rent a room for one night. I came from treatment this morning, and I've been looking since noon for a room for tonight. My bus leaves early in the morning. I know my face looks terrible, but my doctor says with a couple more treatments, I should be okay. I know I look terrible, so I could just sleep on the rocking chair on your porch if you would prefer."

The woman of the house took pity on the man and invited him to eat with the family. "No, thank you," he said, "I have plenty to eat in my paper bag."

After dinner, the woman of the house told him he could have one of the rooms upstairs. He told the family that he was a fisherman and was so grateful for God for allowing him to fish and support his daughter, her crippled husband, and their five children. He also explained that his disfigured face was from a type of skin cancer.

The children of the house loved talking with the little man and were enchanted with his stories of the sea.

The next morning, as he was about to leave the house, he asked if it would be all right to come back when he was in town for his next treatment. The family assured him that he would always be welcomed. He said, "Your children made me feel at home. Grownups are bothered by my face, but children don't seem to mind."

The next time he came to Baltimore for a treatment, he brought a big fish and a quart of large oysters that he had shucked that morning. He arrived at the house by bus at 7 a.m., so the family knew he must have been up at 4 a.m. to prepare this gift.

Over the next few years, he frequently sent fresh fish or oysters or vegetables to the family by mail. The family knew that he had to walk three miles to the nearest post office to mail these treasures.

Then one day, the woman of the house was visiting a friend who had a greenhouse. In it, were beautiful flowers in colorful containers. The most beautiful flower, however, was a golden chrysanthemum in an old rusty bucket. When asked why this beautiful flower was in such a decrepit container, the friend said, "Well, I knew this would be prettiest flower in the whole greenhouse, so I knew it would not mind being in an old rusty container."

The woman thought of the old man, the man with the most inspiring spirit she had ever encountered, living inside a stooped body with an ugly face. And she smiled.

Today as we continue our life journeys this week, it would be a good idea to reflect on how we show mercy to those around us who are in need.

And that is the good news I have for you on this Second Sunday of Easter.

Story source: "The Old Fisherman" in www.frtommylane.com, March 2015.

Chapter 17

3rd Sunday of Easter - B
New Irrational Version

Scripture:

- Acts 3: 13-15, 17-19
- Psalm 4: 2, 4, 7b-8a, 9
- 1 John 2: 1-5a
- Luke 24: 35-48

Today, Catholic Christians celebrate the Third Sunday of Easter.

On this day, we read in the Gospel of Luke how Jesus, after he had risen from the dead, appeared to his disciples and began to teach them. Specifically, we read, "He said to them, 'These are my words that I spoke to you while I was still with you, that everything written about me in the law of Moses and in the prophets and psalms must be fulfilled.' Then he opened their minds to understand the Scriptures. And he said to them, 'Thus it is written that the Christ would suffer and rise from the dead on the third day and that repentance, for the forgiveness of sins, would be preached in his name to all the nations, beginning from Jerusalem. You are witnesses of these things'" (Luke 24: 44-48).

What Jesus was doing with his disciples is called Bible study, the academic field that seeks to answer the question, "What did the original authors of the Bible mean by what they wrote?" Bible study is very different from faith sharing. Unlike Bible study, faith sharing seeks to answer the question, "How does the Scripture touch me personally?"

Bible study, as an academic exercise, can help us appreciate the Bible, for usually the more we know about something, the more we treasure it. Also, Bible study helps us eliminate stray ideas that may have crept into our minds about the Bible, ideas that simply are not true. Children often illustrate this beautifully. Today, I give some actual examples of children's explanation of common Biblical stories and concepts that come from Wayne Rice's *Still More Hot Illustrations for Youth Talks.* Wayne calls this version of the Bible the NIV or New Irrational Version.

> The Bible is full of interesting caricatures. In the first book of the Bible, Guinessis, God got tired of creating the world, so he took the Sabbath off. Adam and Eve were created from an apple tree. One of their children, Cain, asked, "Am I my brother's son?"

> Noah's wife was called Joan of Ark. Noah built an ark, which the animals came to in pears. Lot's wife was a pillar of salt by day, but a ball of fire by night. God asked

Abraham to sacrifice Isaac on Mount Montezuma. Jacob, son of Isaac, stole his brother's birthmark. Jacob was a partridge who had twelve sons. On of Jacob's sons, Joseph, gave refuse to the Israelites.

Sampson was a strong man who let himself be led astray by Jezebel. Then he slayed the Philistines with the ax of the Apostles.

People who lived in Egypt were called mummies. They lived in the Sarah Dessert and traveled by Camelot. The climate of the Sarah is so hot that it is cultivated by irritation. The Egyptians built the Pyramids in the shape of a huge triangular cube. The Pyramids are a range of mountains between France and Spain.

Pharaoh forced the Hebrew slaves to make bread without straw. Moses led the Hebrews to the Red Sea, where they made unleavened bread, which is bread without any ingredients. The Egyptians were all drowned in the dessert. Afterward, Moses went up to Mount Cyanide to get the Ten Amendments. The First Commandment was when Eve told Adam to eat the apple. The Fifth Commandment is humor thy father and mother. The Seventh Commandment is thou shalt not admit adultery.

Moses died before he ever reached Canada. Then Joshua led the Hebrews in the battle of Geritol. The greatest miracle in the Bible is when Joshua told his son to stand still and he obeyed him.

David was a Hebrew king skilled at playing the liar. He fought with the Finkelsteins, a race of people who lived in Biblical times. Solomon, one of David's sons, had 300 wives and 700 porcupines.

When Mary heard that she was the Mother of Jesus, she sang the Magna Carta. When the three wise guys from the east side arrived, they found Jesus in the Manger. Jesus was born because Mary had an immaculate contraption. St. John, the blacksmith, dumped water on his head.

The people who followed the Lord were called the twelve decibels. The epistles were the wives of the apostles. One of the opossums was St. Matthew, who was by profession a taxi man. St. Paul cavorted to Christianity. He preached holy acrimony, which is another name for marriage. A Christian should have only one. This is called monotony.

Though these illustrations are definitely humorous, they are excellent examples of how we can misinterpret the Scriptures if we are not careful. Such misinterpretation is not only common among children, but it is seen frequently among adults.

As we continue our life journeys this week, it would be good idea to reflect on our own relationship to the Bible. How faithful are we to studying it and treasuring it?

And that is the good news I have for you on this Third Sunday of Easter.

Story source: Anonymous, "The New Irrational Version (NIV)," in Wayne Rice (Ed.), *Still More Hot Illustrations for Youth Talks*. Grand Rapids, Michigan: Zondervan/Youth Specialties, 1999, pp. 104-106.

Chapter 18

4th Sunday of Easter 4 - B
The Butcher

Scripture:

- Acts 4: 8-12
- Psalm 118: 1 & 8-9, 21-23, 26 & 21 & 29
- 1 John 3: 1-2
- John 10: 11-18

Today, Catholic Christians celebrate the Fourth Sunday of Easter, sometimes called Good Shepherd Sunday.

On this day, in the Gospel of John, we hear Jesus say, "I am the good shepherd. A good shepherd lays down his life for the sheep" (John 10: 11).

Seeing Jesus as a good shepherd, and human beings as his sheep is a beautiful image. Unlike many animals, sheep cannot protect themselves. They are totally dependent on a shepherd for their safety from enemies such as wolves. Because of this, they put all their trust in the shepherd.

Another interesting thing about sheep is that they follow the shepherd because they know him. They recognize his voice, and so they follow him. They don't follow strangers whose voices they don't recognize.

That is the message that a tour guide was trying to communicate to some fellow tourists he had accompanied on a trip to the Holy Land. Unfortunately, however, something happened to ruin the lesson plan. Lynn Anderson tells the story in his book, *They Smell like Sheep* (Howard Publishing Company, 1997).

Several years ago, Lynn and his wife Carolyn were traveling in Palestine with fellow tourists. As they traveled through the countryside, they were enchanted by the scenery, history and lifestyle of the people as told by the tour guide. In his description, the tour guide engaged in a heart-warming portrayal of the relationship of a shepherd with his sheep. The guide told the people that a shepherd feeds the sheep with care, and how he is always gentle with them.

The guide pointed out that because the shepherd leads the sheep, instead of driving them, there is never any reason for the shepherd to be harsh with the sheep. The sheep love and trust the shepherd, and the shepherd loves his sheep.

The tour guide went on to say that on a past tour, he was telling the tourists the same message about the beautiful relationship between shepherd and sheep. In the middle of his pastoral tale, however, he suddenly lost his audience. All of them were looking out one side of the bus' windows at a man chasing a herd of sheep. He was throwing rocks at them, whacking them with sticks, and siccing the sheep dog on them. The sheep-driving man in the field had completely torpedoed the guide's enchanting narrative.

The tour guide told his audience how he had become so angry, that he jumped out of the bus, ran to the man chasing the sheep, and accosted him. The guide said, "Do you know what you have just done? I was spinning a charming story about how gentle shepherds are and how the sheep love him. And here you are, mistreating and assaulting these sheep. What is going on? Just what kind of a no-good shepherd are you!"

The man looked bewildered for a minute and then replied, "Shepherd? Shepherd! I'm not the shepherd! I'm the butcher!"

The poor butcher taught the tourists what a shepherd is by showing them the opposite of what a shepherd is.

From the Scripture and the story of the butcher, we can glean some important things. Here are just three of them.

First, just as sheep need to learn to recognize their shepherd, we as Christians need to know our shepherd. And for us, Jesus is our Good Shepherd. Therefore, to truly be able to follow him, we need to know him. We do this by reading the Sacred Scripture passages of the New Testament, paying special attention to what he taught. We need to recognize the commandments he taught, commandments such as welcoming the stranger, giving drink to the thirsty, feeding the hungry, sheltering the homeless, instructing the ignorant, consoling the sorrowful, caring for the sick, visiting those in prison, burying the dead, praying for others, and treating others as we would like to be treated.

Second, though we say we recognize Jesus as the Good Shepherd, we must also be careful not to be led astray by those who are not Jesus. Some people, for example, are very susceptible to religious leaders who are television personalities or who have fancy titles or positions, especially such characters inside the Catholic Church. Others are susceptible to gifted preachers with sparkling personalities and words and settings that dazzle. Others are led astray by political figures that are actually wolves in sheep's clothing, using a phrase from Jesus here and there to trick others into thinking they are advocating something that Jesus, the prince of love, would advocate.

And third, to be a follower of the Shepherd, we need to evaluate everything we receive in light of the triple-love command of Jesus Christ – to love God, to love others, as we love ourselves. If a message we receive does not show love to others, God, or self, we must reject it. For if we accept anti-love messages as something good, we have, in effect, shown our disdain for the Good Shepherd and all he stands for.

As we continue our life journeys this week, it would be a good idea to reflect on Jesus as Good Shepherd. How does the image of the Good Shepherd speak to our hearts? How do we know him, and how do we follow him?

And that is the good news I have for you on this Fourth Sunday of Easter.

Story source: "They Smell like Sheep," contributed by Jason Jones in Sermon Central (WWW), April 2015. The story comes from Lynn Anderson's book, *They Smell like Sheep*, Howard Publishing Company, 1997.

Chapter 19

5th Sunday of Easter - B
A Bike for Jerry

Scripture:

- Acts 9: 26-31
- Psalm 22: 26b-27, 28 & 30, 31-32
- 1 John 3: 18-24
- John 15: 1-8

Today, Catholic Christians celebrate the Fifth Sunday of Easter.

On this day, we read in the First Letter of John, "Children, let us love not in word or speech, but in deed and truth" (1 John 3: 18).

In modern American English, we have certain expressions related to this concept. We say, for example, "Talk is cheap." That means that it is very easy to say we'll do something, but it is much more difficult to actually do it. Or, we may say, "Put your money where your mouth is." This means that if we truly believe in something, we will readily invest in it with our time, talent, and/or treasure. Even St. James wrote of putting our words into deeds when he said, "Faith, without works, is dead" (James 2: 26).

Love, in theology, means wishing the best for ourselves and for others. In a religious context, love is not an emotional state of being. Rather, it is a function of our intellect.

In Catholic Christianity, we have specific lists of how we can show love in concrete ways, known as the "spiritual and corporal works of mercy."

But it is also a good idea, from time to time, to consider the examples of ordinary people around us who are putting their love for others in practical, concrete ways. For as a result of their actions, they become like shining lamps, spreading light in a sea of darkness, models for the rest of us to follow.

In the following story, called "A Bike for Jerry," writer Roberta Donovan tells of a man who did put his faith into action. His name was Bud.

Bud Lee was a retired farmer who lived in Denton, Montana. Frequently, he walked past the house of a little boy named Jerry Clark. As he walked, he would see little Jerry looking out the window, watching other children playing outside. Jerry was paralyzed from the waist down from a birth injury. Bud could tell from the look on the little boy's face how much he wished he could be outside playing with them also.

Then one day, Jerry's mother, Barbara, brought Bud a picture of a hand-operated bicycle that she had found in a magazine. She said, "It is just the thing for Jerry, but it is no longer manufactured. Do you think you could build a hand-operated bicycle for Jerry?"

Bud was not surprised by Barbara's request, because after his retirement, he had set up a little repair shop. Though he set up the shop as "just a place to tinker," people around town said that Bud could build anything.

A hand-operated bicycle, however, was a very ambitious project. He had no design, so every little step was by trial-and-error. He bought some of the parts, and he salvaged other parts from old bicycles. Gradually, with much care, patience, and ingenuity, Bud had built a chain-driven, hand-powered, three-wheeled "bike" for little Jerry.

When it was all done, the Clark family was delighted, especially Jerry. Now, the little boy could go outside and join the other children. He didn't have to sit by the window, looking out, watching the world pass him by. Now, he could be an active participant in the life around him.

Soon, other parents of children with disabilities began contacting Bud to ask for his help. Before he knew it, he had built more than twenty special bicycles. Each bicycle took him about two weeks to build. Three of them he sent to Shriners Hospitals for Children, and others went to children in nine other states. And when little Jerry grew out of his bicycle, Bud made him a new one.

Bud refused to accept even a penny for his bicycles even though he bought most of the parts by himself. Whenever people tried to pay him, he would say something similar to what he told Jerry's family, "The look on Jerry's face as he rides down the sidewalk is all the payment I need."

Stories like this are not only inspirational, but they also serve to guide our own behavior. Such stories, coupled with the Scripture passages we read about love, can teach us many things. Here are three.

First, to love is a Christian commandment. In fact, the triple love command of Jesus Christ is the foundation for how we are to live our lives. This commandment is seen in many passages of the New Testament (Matthew 22: 37-39; Mark 12: 30-34; Luke 10: 27).

Second, the love that Jesus was referring to has nothing to do with an emotional state. On the contrary, it is based on our intellect. We help others not because we have emotional ties to them, but simply because it is what we are called to do as Christians. We wish the best for our self and for others, and we put this wish into action.

And third, love is a virtue, and virtues are habits. Therefore, the more we practice a virtue, the more ingrained and easy it becomes in our lives. In time, practicing the virtue becomes "second-nature" to us.

As we continue our life journeys this week, it would be a good idea to reflect on how we love God, others, and our selves. How could we strengthen this virtue?

And that is the good news I have for you on this Fifth Sunday of Easter.

Story source: Roberta Donovan, "A Bike for Jerry," in *Friends in Deed: Stories About Acts of Kindness – A Guideposts Book,* Nashville, Tennessee, Dimensions for Living, 1997, pp. 74-75.

Chapter 20

6th Sunday of Easter - B
Sr. Carla Piette, M.M.

Scripture:

- Acts 10: 25-26, 34-35, 44-48
- Psalm 98: 1, 2-3ab, 3cd-4
- 1 John 4: 7-10
- John 15: 9-17

Today, Catholic Christians celebrate the Sixth Sunday of Easter.

On this day, in the Gospel of John we hear Jesus telling his disciples, "This is my commandment: love one another as I love you. No one has greater love than this, to lay down one's life for one's friends" (John 15: 12-13).

For over 2,000 years, the Catholic Church has treasured those who have given their lives in the service of the Church and those who have shed their blood as martyrs. In fact, in the early days of the Church, only martyrs were considered worthy of being called "saints."

For most of us, "laying down one's life for one's friends" is something we only read about and will never experience it in our everyday lives.

Today, we look at the life of a heroic woman who gave her life so that her friend could live. Her name was Carla Piette.

When she was 19-years old and a student at Marquette University, Carla decided to become a Maryknoll Missionary Sister. Her superiors described her as "...friendly, outgoing, jovial, big-hearted and generous, but rather naïve and tactless."

Carla was also at times very anti-clerical. She didn't care if a person was a priest or a bishop; she refused to treat priests or bishops with any special deference for their vocational status. But, as we will see, she did admire people who preached a Gospel of love, especially those who were champions of the poor.

Carla served as a missionary in Chile from 1964 to 1979. During her time there, she worked with the poorest of the poor. Though she suffered from depression from time to time, she had a very strong inner core that allowed her to serve God by serving others day after day. One of her biographers, Jacqueline Hansen Maggiore, described Carla as a "... teacher, parish leader, prophet, clown, poet and scripture scholar."

In 1973, Carla made friends with another Maryknoll Sister named Ita Ford. During these years, Chile experienced great turmoil. President Allende was killed and soldiers filled the streets. The dictator Augusto Pinochet and government death squads killed tens of thousands of people. Over 300 Catholic missionaries and priests were ordered out of the country, and at least three were killed.

After serving in Chile, both Carla and Ita took a break. But they were not happy being back in the United States, for they knew the great needs of the people in Central and South American nations.

In 1980, both Carla and Ita heard the call of an amazing man named Oscar Romero, the Archbishop of San Salvador. He called on Church workers from other nations to come and help the Church in El Salvador, which was experiencing incredible persecution.

Astonishingly, Sr. Carla arrived in El Salvador on the day the Archbishop was martyred, and Sr. Ita arrived in El Salvador on the day of his funeral. Little did they know that their times on earth were also soon to end.

Carla and Ita were so close as friends and coworkers that people began calling them "Carla y Ita" – Carla and Ita – which in Spanish sounds like one word – "Carlita" or "Little Carla."

In El Salvador, they found themselves in the middle of a war, a war against the poor. They did their best to bury the dead, help priests escape, feed the poor, console those in sorrow, and serve refugees. Every day, both Sisters knew that they might be the next to lose their lives.

On August 22, 1980, Sr. Carla wrote to a friend, "We dally along in this crazy circus of life where so often the Divine Circus Master doesn't clue us into the act for tomorrow yet always gives us the strength to perform. . . . I leave the future in the Circus Master's hands."

One day later, on August 23, 1980, Sisters Carla and Ita were helping a man who had just been released from prison, escorting him to his town. After delivering him, they were on their way back home when a flash flood engulfed them in water. Carla, who was big and strong, lifted the petite Ita and pushed her out of the window. Miraculously, Sr. Ita was saved, but Sr. Carla drowned. She gave her life for her friend.

Though Sr. Ita lived, it was not for long. In early December of 1980, Maryknoll Sisters Ita Ford and Maura Clarke, along with two missionaries from Cleveland – Ursuline Sister Dorothy Kazel and Maryknoll Lay Missionary Jean Donovan – were martyred for the faith.

Though many people have heard of the four women martyrs of El Salvador, fewer know the inspirational story of Maryknoll Sister Carla Piette. That is a shame, for it is good to know that despite all the problems of the world today, there are people willing to lay down their lives for their friends.

As we continue our life journeys this week, it would be a good idea to reflect on the remarkable Carla and people like her. Would we be willing to give our lives for our friends?

And that is the good news I have for you on this Sixth Sunday of Easter.

Story sources:

- "Carla Piette, Presente!" by John Dear, October 19, 2010, World Wide Web.
- "Servants of God," in Penny Lernoux, *Hearts on Fire: The Story of the Maryknoll Sisters,* Maryknoll, N.Y., Orbis Books, 1993, pp. 224-241.
- Maggiore, Jacqueline Hansen, *Vessel of Clay: The Inspirational Journey of Sister Carla, Scranton,* Pennsylvania, University of Scranton Press, 2010.

Chapter 21

Ascension - B
Brother Joseph Dutton

Scripture:

- Acts 1: 1-11
- Psalm 47: 2-3, 6-7, 8-9
- Ephesians 4: 1-13
- Mark 16: 15-20

Today, Catholic Christians celebrate the feast of the Ascension of Jesus.

On this day, we read the command Jesus gave to his disciples to become missionaries when he said, "Go into the whole world and proclaim the gospel to every creature" (Mark 16: 15). We call this the "commissioning" of the apostles.

For over 2,000 years, Catholic Christians have, indeed, gone into the world to proclaim the good news of Jesus Christ. Today, we look at the humble but inspirational life of a lay missionary named Ira Barnes Dutton.

Ira was born into a Protestant household on April 27, 1843 in Stowe, Vermont. When he was 18 years old, Ira was living in Wisconsin. There, he taught Sunday school and worked in a bookstore. Ira also liked to write about his life in journals.

When the Civil War broke out, Ira wrote of his excitement. In September of 1861, he enlisted in the Thirteenth Wisconsin Infantry Regiment, fighting for the Union. Even though his regiment did not have many combat experiences, he rose to the rank of Captain.

Ira was discharged in 1866, because after the war there was less need for people of his military rank.

When he got out of the army, Ira married a woman notorious for her promiscuity. His friends warned him against the marriage, but he wouldn't listen to them. In a short time, Ira discovered that his friends had been right. His wife cheated on him and was a shopaholic. Not only did she run away with another man, but also she spent all of Ira's money. Ira kept hoping that one day she would return to him, but she never did. So he finally divorced her in 1881.

During the next two decades, Ira had many jobs. He worked in cemeteries, oversaw a distillery in Alabama, and worked on railroads in Memphis. In 1875, he joined the War Department, settling claims against the government.

Though he was a good worker, Ira was what today we would call a "functioning alcoholic." Every night and weekend, he would drink alcohol to excess. In 1876, however, he was so ashamed of his double life that he vowed never to drink again. This pledge he kept for the rest of his life. At his death, he could claim 55 years of continuous sobriety.

In 1883, on his fortieth birthday, Ira became a Catholic Christian and changed his name from "Ira" to "Joseph" in honor of his favorite saint.

Joseph then retired from government and set out to begin a new life. He wanted this new life to be one of penance for what he called his "wild years" and "sinful capers."

The first thing he did in his new life was to live at the Trappist monastery of Our Lady of Gethsemani in Kentucky for 20 months. But he concluded that to serve God more fully, he should live an active, apostolic life instead of a contemplative one. It was at this time that Joseph heard about the famous Father Damien who was working with lepers on the island of Molokai, one of the Hawaiian Islands. He determined to give his life to help Fr. Damien.

In 1886, three years before Fr. Damien died, Joseph arrived, filled with the zeal that all missionaries feel when they begin their ministries. This intense missionary fire never left him.

Joseph soon found his way into the hearts of the people of Molokai. And though he never took vows as a religious brother, people began calling him "Brother Joseph." They soon began relying on him for many things. Joseph was a jack-of-all-trades. In other words, he did what needed to be done. If Fr. Damien needed an administrator, Brother Joseph would be an administrator. Sometimes he would be a carpenter. Other times, he would assist nurses in caring for the sick. Other time he would be a repairman or a basketball coach or simply a consoler of the sick and dying.

Just before he died, Fr. Damien – who is now known as Saint Damien – told everyone that he could die in peace knowing that Brother Joseph was on hand to take his place.

And Brother Joseph did continue Fr. Damien's work, and joyfully. In fact, he was known for being a jovial and peaceful person. When he was 83 years old, Joseph wrote in his journal that his natural inclination was to be jolly. He reported that he was always ready to laugh, that a laugh was always just waiting to break out.

When people would ask him if he would like to take a vacation, he dismissed the idea. To him, no place could be as happy or fulfilling as working on Molokai. For him, a vacation would be more like a form of slavery.

Brother Joseph served the people of Molokai faithfully and joyfully for 45 years. Before his death, he wrote, "It has been a happy place – a happy life."

Today, many people are working toward Brother Joseph's canonization. And of all the things we can learn from his life, to me the most important is that peace and joy come from doing God's will. When we truly love what we are doing, and it is in harmony with God's will for us, how could we not live a happy and holy life?

And that is the good news I have for you on this Feast of the Ascension.

Story sources:

- Heu, Olena, "The Path to Sainthood: Brother Joseph Dutton," published April 10, 2014. (World Wide Web).
- McNamara, Pat, "A Servant of the Lepers: Brother Joseph of Molokai," Patheos.com, October 8, 2012.

Chapter 22

Pentecost - B
The Puppy

Scripture:

- Acts 2: 1-11
- Psalm 104: 1ab & 24ac, 29bc-30, 31 & 34
- Galatians 5: 16-25
- John 15: 26-27; 16: 12-15

Today, Catholic Christians celebrate the feast of Pentecost, the birthday of the Catholic Church in particular, and of Christianity in general.

On this day, we celebrate the day when the Holy Spirit came down upon the early disciples, bringing them many gifts. Previously afraid and confused, they were given an abundance of courage, zeal, knowledge, wisdom, and other virtues necessary to become vibrant and effective missionaries throughout the world.

In St. Paul's First Letter to the Corinthians, we read, "There are different kinds of spiritual gifts but the same Spirit; there are different forms of service but the same Lord; there are different workings but the same God who produces all of them in everyone. To each individual the manifestation of the Spirit is given for some benefit" (1 Corinthians 12: 4-7).

It takes many people with different gifts to build up the Kingdom of God on earth. Sometimes, however, when we look at others' gifts and feel they are lacking in ourselves, we lose heart and come to believe we have nothing to offer. That is faulty thinking, for every one of us, as Christians, has gifts to offer for the benefit of all. That is what a puppy discovered to his delight in a fable by John Aikin.

There was once a little puppy who lived on a farm. One day, when he was old enough to walk around by himself, he decided to take a tour of the farm to learn more about the place.

He first came to an area where a horse was eating. The big animal called to the little puppy and said, "You must be new here. You'll soon discover that the master loves me more than all the other animals here on the farm because I can carry heavy loads for him. I suspect that an animal of your size is of no value to him at all."

The little puppy hung his head in shame, for he knew that was true. He would never be big enough or strong enough to carry heavy loads for the master. But just as he was about to walk away, a cow in the next pen called out to him. The cow said, "Don't believe the horse, because I have the most honored position on the farm. You see, I give milk, and the farmer's wife makes cheese and butter from my milk. You, of course, provide nothing of value to the family."

The puppy was crushed. As he was about to leave, a sheep began to speak. "Listen, Cow, your position is no greater than mine. I provide wool so that the family can have clothes. My wool provides blankets so the whole family can keep warm on winter nights. However, I do agree with you about dogs. They give the master nothing."

As the puppy walked along, all of the animals of the farm joined in the conversation, telling the puppy how great they were because of the fine gifts they were able to give for the master and his family. The chicken, for example, told how her eggs fed the family, and the cat told how she was excellent at chasing away mice because of her gift of swiftness. Every animal agreed that dogs provided no value to the family or its farm.

The puppy was crushed. He walked away from the other animals and found a quiet, secluded place to cry. As he cried, an old dog heard his sobs and asked him what was wrong. The puppy told the old dog about what the other animals said. "They are right," he said, "I provide no service to anyone."

The old dog said, "Well, it's true that you'll never produce milk, eggs, or wool, and certainly you'll never be as good cats in chasing away mice or carrying heavy loads like horses. However, you have the gift of bringing laughter and cheer to people. I'll show you what I mean when the master comes home from working all day in the fields." The old dog then told the puppy how to act when he saw his master at the end of the day.

That evening, when the master came home, the little puppy ran to him, licked his feet, and jumped into his arms. Falling to the ground, the farmer romped with the puppy in the grass. Finally, he held him to his chest and, patting him on the head, said, "No matter how tired I am when I get home, I feel better when you greet me. I wouldn't trade you for all the animals on the farm."

This story, along with the readings from First Corinthians, tells us some very important things. Here are three.

First, God gives gifts to each of us.

Second, many of our gifts are social in nature. That means that we are to share them with others. By doing this, we help build up the Kingdom of God on earth.

And third, we should not minimize our gifts or their value. Not everyone is called to be a missionary in a war-torn zone. Not everyone is called to be a martyr. Not everyone is called to be an ordained priest. So what! What is important is that we treasure our gifts, develop them, and share them abundantly with joy.

As we continue our life journeys on this Feast of Pentecost, it would be a good idea to reflect on our gifts. How do we treasure them and expand them? How do we put them into action to build up the Kingdom of God on earth as we are called to do as missionaries?

And that is the good news I have for you on this Feast of Pentecost.

Story source:

- "The Little Dog," a story adapted from a fable by John Aikin, in William R. White (Ed.), *Stories for Telling: A Treasury for Christian Storytellers, Minneapolis*, MN, Augsburg Publishing House, 1986, pp. 41-42.

Part Three

ORDINARY TIME

Chapter 23

Holy Trinity - B
St. Katharine Drexel

Scripture:

- Deuteronomy 4: 32-34, 39-40
- Psalm 33: 4-5, 6 & 9, 18-19, 20 & 22
- Romans 8: 14-17
- Matthew 28: 16-20

This Sunday, Catholic Christians throughout the world celebrate the Feast of the Most Holy Trinity.

Though the concept of "Trinity" is not specifically mentioned in the books of the Bible, Catholic Christians, like most Christians, believe in God the Father, God the Son, and God the Holy Spirit. This dogma holds that though there is only one God, there are three Divine Persons in this one God.

We see God the Father, who is often simply called "God," as the Creator of the Universe. We see God the Son, who came down to Earth and took a human form called Jesus, as our Redeemer or Savior. And we see God the Holy Spirit as the Sanctifier and Gift Giver.

In today's Gospel reading, we hear Jesus tell his disciples, "All power in heaven and on earth has been given to me. Go, therefore, and make disciples of all nations, baptizing them in the name of the Father, and of the Son, and of the Holy Spirit, teaching them to observe all that I have commanded you. And behold, I am with you always, until the end of the age" (Matthew 28: 18-20).

Many Christians, when they read this passage today, say to themselves, "Well, what's the problem? This is clear as a bell. There is God the Father, Son, and Holy Spirit. How could you not know there is a Triune God?" Well, it took centuries for the Church to develop the dogma of the Trinity. What we believe today is the result of much theological "unpacking" of Sacred Scripture, Church councils, and plenty of strife.

One thing that the Catholic Church did not need centuries to grasp, however, was the missionary mandate of Jesus Christ. From the time of Pentecost, when the Holy Spirit brought the early disciples the spiritual gifts necessary to be effective missionaries, the Church has sent many men and women to spread the Good News of Jesus Christ to the whole world. Many missionaries left their native land to spread the good news in countries foreign to them.

Some people, however, saw a need to do missionary work in their own lands. Today, we examine the life of one such person named Katharine Drexel.

Katharine was born on November 26, 1858 in Philadelphia, Pennsylvania. Her family was very rich. They were also very generous with their time, talent and treasure. Her mother opened her home to the poor three days each week, and her father spent at least a half-hour in prayer every evening.

As a rich heiress, Katharine had the finest education money could buy, and she traveled widely. Katharine, however, had two experiences in life that had a profound impact on her.

First, she watched her stepmother die from cancer. She realized that all the money in the world could not buy happiness and security.

Second, she developed a passion for Native American Indians. She was especially touched by a book by Helen Hunt Jackson called *A Century of Dishonor* about the plight of American Indians. Then, on a trip to the western states in 1884, Katharine saw the great needs of these poor people.

So, on a trip to Italy in 1887, Katharine and her family had a private audience with Pope Leo XIII. When she asked the pope if he would send missionaries to help Indian missions that she had been supporting in the western United States, the pope surprised her by saying, "Why don't you become a missionary?"

And that is exactly what Katharine did. She founded a religious order of women called the Sisters of the Blessed Sacrament for Indians and Colored. She knew that like Native American Indians, African-Americans were also victims of prejudice and discrimination. Though she and her sisters suffered much at the hands of the Ku Klux Klan and other disciples of hate, they persevered.

By 1943, Mother Katharine had founded black Catholic schools in 13 states, 50 missions for Indians in 16 states, and another 40 mission centers and 23 rural schools.

The institution she is most famous for founding, however, is Xavier University in New Orleans, the first Catholic university in the United States principally for African-Americans.

In addition to her focus on Indians and African-Americans, Katharine was a very generous woman, always willing to give money to worthy causes. One of these causes was providing money to buy land on which to build a Catholic church in Wilmington, North Carolina. Today, on the piece of land that Katharine Drexel bought, sits the Basilica Shrine of St. Mary. This parish, which has always been a beacon of hope to the poor and a welcome home to the immigrant, continues its missionary mandate on the Cape Fear Coast of North Carolina and in the mountains of Honduras.

Katharine Drexel died in 1955 and was canonized in 2000, the second saint born in the United States. St. Katharine Drexel's feast day is March 3.

As we continue our life journeys this week, it would be a good idea to reflect on the men and women who gave their lives to home missions. What kind of missionary work can we do in our own land?

And that is the good news I have for you on this Feast of the Most Holy Trinity.

Story sources:

- "St. Katharine Drexel (1858-1955)," Saint of the Day/*Saints & Angels*.
- "Blessed Katharine Drexel," In *Butler's Lives of the Saints: New Full Edition: March*, Revised by Teresa Rodrigues, O.S.B., The Liturgical Press/ Burns & Oates, 1999, pp. 20-22.

Chapter 24

Holy Body & Blood of Christ - B
The Bridge Keeper

Scripture:

- Exodus 24: 3-8
- Psalm 116: 12-13, 15 & 16 bc, 17-18
- Hebrews 9: 11-15
- Mark 14: 12-16, 22-26

Today, Catholic Christians celebrate the feast of the Most Holy Body and Blood of Christ, sometimes called *Corpus Christi*.

Unlike Holy Thursday, the day on which we celebrate the whole Eucharist or Mass, today's feast celebrates just one part of the Eucharist – the Blessed Sacrament or Holy Communion. Most importantly, it reminds us of the real presence of Jesus in the consecrated elements of bread and wine. For Catholic Christians, once the ordained priest or bishop consecrates the bread and wine at Mass, the bread and wine become transformed into Jesus' actual body and blood. In other words, though the bread and wine *look* the same, their *essence* has changed into Christ.

The change of bread and wine into Christ is important, for it reminds us of the nature of sacrifice. In the Old Testament, for example, people offered sacrifices to honor God, seal covenants or promises, or to remove sin. For the sacrifice to be effective, the element that was offered to God had to be changed. In today's reading from Exodus, for example, people offered animals to God by killing them. When people offered items like grain, it was burned. Today, sometimes, people write down their sins or things they are ashamed of on little pieces of paper, and burn them to symbolize the destruction of the old and the birth of the new.

Jesus himself was considered a sacrifice. Christians sometimes call Jesus the "paschal lamb," the pure, innocent lamb destroyed for our salvation. Like the paschal lamb, the perfect lamb used in the highest of all Hebrew feasts – Passover – Jesus is destroyed so we may live.

Today's feast also reminds us that for over 2,000 years, Catholic Christians have followed the command of Jesus to continue celebrating this ritual. I'll say more about that later. For now, however, let's look at an amazing story about a bridge keeper who sacrificed his son so that others could live.

There was once a "swing bridge" that spanned a large river. During most of the day and night, the bridge was aligned with the river, parallel to the banks. This allowed ships to pass up and down the river. But at certain times of the day, the bridge would be rotated across the river so that a train could cross.

A bridge keeper sat in a little shack where he operated the bridge and locked it into place when a train came. One evening, the bridge keeper heard the train coming and caught sight of the train lights in the distance. He stepped to the control and turned the bridge into position.

Unfortunately, however, the electrical control did not work this time. The bridge would not lock automatically. The bridge keeper knew that if he did not get the bridge to lock, the train would crash and kill many people. Therefore, he ran to the other side of the bridge to manually lock the bridge. The only way he could get the bridge safely locked was to stand and hold a lever until the train had safely gone over the river.

As he waited for the oncoming train, he heard a sound that made his blood turn cold. His four-year old son was calling out, "Daddy, where are you?" The bridge keeper knew the little boy was on the train tracks, and that the train would be crossing any minute. He wanted to call out to the little boy to run, but he knew that the boy's tiny legs would never allow him to cross the bridge to safety.

The bridge keeper almost left the lever to run to snatch up his son and carry him to safety, but he realized that he could not get back to the lever on time to save the train. Either his son or the people on the train must die. He took a moment to make his decision.

The bridge keeper kept his hand on the lever. The train sped by safely and swiftly. Nobody on board the train knew that the tiny body of the little boy had been thrown mercilessly in the river by the train. Nor were they aware of the sobbing father, pitiful in his grief, still clinging tightly to the locking lever long after the train had passed. Nor did anyone see the poor father walking home more slowly than he had ever walked, to tell his wife how their son had been brutally killed.

Some people have asked, through the centuries, why Catholic Christians "duplicate" the passion of Jesus. The fact is, we do not "duplicate" Christ's passion and death. Once was sufficient. Therefore, if someone asks you how many Masses have ever been offered" the answer is "One." When we come to celebrate the Eucharist, we mystically enter the one and only one passion, death, and resurrection of Jesus.

On today's feast day, we are asked to give thanks for the miracle of the Blessed Sacrament – Jesus really present under the appearance of bread and wine. And to know that the Blessed Sacrament is present, Catholic Churches have a sanctuary lamp lit.

As we continue our life journeys this week, it would be a good idea to give thanks for the gift of the Blessed Sacrament, the gift that Jesus gave us over 2,000 years ago.

And that is the good news I have for you on this Feast of the Most Holy Body and Blood of Christ.

Story source:

- Anonymous, "The Bridge Keeper," in www.inspirationaslarchive. com, June, 2015

Chapter 25

2nd Sunday in Ordinary Time - B
Sisters Jane & Mary Lou

Scripture:

- 1 Samuel 3: 3b-10, 19
- Psalm 40: 2 & 4ab, 7-8a, 8b-9, 10
- 1 Corinthians 6: 13c-15a, 17-20
- John 1: 35-42

Today, Catholic Christians celebrate the Second Sunday in Ordinary Time. On this day, we read about hearing and responding to God's call. In the First Book of Samuel, for example, we hear God calling Samuel. Samuel, who was very eager to serve the Lord, said, "Speak, for your servant is listening" (1 Samuel 3: 10). And in the Gospel of John, we hear how two brothers, Andrew and Simon, heard Jesus call them and followed him (John 1: 40-42).

All of us who have been baptized have been called by God to follow Jesus.

At our baptism, the Holy Spirit entered into us, making us anointed ministers of the Church. We frequently call this process becoming part of the "priesthood of all believers."

Although we all receive gifts of the Holy Spirit, each of us receives special talents, dreams, passions, and abilities. Each of us is called to build up the Kingdom of God here on earth. We do this by serving God by serving others.

Most of us are familiar with the vocation of parents who serve God by raising children. Today, I wish to give you a glimpse into a different vocation, that of two Maryknoll Missionary Sisters who work in Guatemala. They are Sister Jane and Sister Mary Lou.

Sr. Jane, from Milwaukee, heard the call of God to serve him as a Religious Sister when she was a teenager. She entered the Maryknoll Sisters at the age of 18 and calls herself a "child bride." After she became a Maryknoll Sister, Jane studied to become a medical doctor, and later did her surgical residency to become a surgeon. She went to Guatemala in 1963 and has been serving there since that time except for four years in the United States serving on her congregation's leadership team.

Sr. Mary Lou, a native of Detroit, became a physician first and later became a religious sister. After she finished her surgical residency, she spent a year as an emergency room physician in Miami. After she became a Maryknoll Missionary Sister, she went to Guatemala in 1981 and has been serving there continuously except for six years serving her congregation's leadership team in the United States.

Today, the Sisters work in the Department of San Marcos, Guatemala. There, they have a clinic in a town called Catarina. At this clinic, which I visited in 2011, the Sisters serve the poor. Because they have been there for many years, the people trust them. The people know that the Sisters will be there for them and can be counted on. Sister Jane – or "Just call me Jane!" – has been there for about 50 years. She has been there before most of her clients were even on the planet!

On Mondays, the clinic is filled with patients waiting to be helped. The Sisters treat diabetes, upper respiratory infections, tropical diseases, AIDS, and the whole range of other maladies that people can have. In children, one of the biggest problems the Sisters encounter is malnutrition caused by poverty.

From Tuesday through Friday, the Sisters leave the clinic in Catarina and go to the rural villages. While they are gone, health promoters keep the clinic open for filling prescriptions and treating patients with minor complaints.

One of the most fascinating accomplishments of the Sisters is a program to train people as health promoters. These people receive a series of six, four-day training sessions. They then go back to their rural villages where they provide basic health services to their friends and neighbors – always at zero cost. The health promoters, who are both men and women, can do first aid, care for pregnant women, give vaccinations, prescribe basic medications, and teach sound health principles. Without them, people in the remote villages would have no health care at all.

In a recent article in *Maryknoll Magazine* (January/February 2014, pp. 46-50), Sr. Jane said,

"My focus was mission from the start, and I think it's the blending of the two (mission and being a doctor) that has allowed me to stay 50 years. The early 1980s were the worst years, but we always thought we could take more because the folks could take more, so how could you take less? If it wasn't for the Gospel, I couldn't be here!" (p. 50).

Though Sisters Jane and Mary Lou have very specialized vocations, all of us are called to follow the Lord in various ways. Here are three things we must always keep in mind.

First, we all have gifts and talents from the Lord.

Second, as Christians, we are called to build up the Kingdom of God here on earth. We do this by serving God by serving others.

And third, all gifts are social in nature. We do not receive gifts to be hoarded; they are to be shared. Even those who are called to the recluse and hermit vocations are called to pray for others.

As we continue our life journeys this week, it would be a good idea to reflect on our own vocation journeys. What is God calling us to do with our gifts? How are we responding?

And that is the good news I have for you on this Second Sunday in Ordinary Time.

Story source: Sprague, Sean, "Miracles in Catarina," *Maryknoll Magazine*, January/February 2014, pp. 46-50.

Chapter 26

3rd Sunday in Ordinary Time - B
St. Joseph Calasanz

Scripture:

- Jonah 3: 1-5, 10
- Psalm 25: 4-5ab, 6 & 7bc, 8-9
- 1 Corinthians 7: 29-31
- Mark 1: 14-20

Today, Catholic Christians celebrate the Third Sunday in Ordinary Time.

On this day, we hear Jesus saying, "Repent, and believe in the gospel" (Mark 1: 15). This is the same phrase we will hear in a few weeks when we receive ashes on our foreheads on Ash Wednesday.

In today's Gospel selection, we also hear the call of Simon and his brother Andrew, and the Zebedee brothers – James and John. All of them followed Jesus immediately at his invitation to become "fishers of men" (Mark 1: 17). We heard this call of Simon and Andrew last week in the Gospel of John.

All of us are called by the Lord to build up the Kingdom of God here on earth and to share the good news of Jesus with others. Though we are all called to the basic vocation of Christian, we are also called at various points on our life journeys to do some specific things. Though most follow Jesus by becoming parents and raising children, some are called to be priests, Brothers, or Sisters in the Church. That is the vocational journey of a man named Joseph Calasanz, a Spanish saint who lived from 1557 to 1648.

Joseph was born in the Kingdom of Aragon, Spain, youngest of eight children. He had an excellent education and, at the age of 14, he decided he would become a priest one day. He obtained a Doctor of Laws degree from the University of Lleida and then did theological studies at two Spanish universities: the University of Valencia and at Complutense University. Despite his father's desire for him to get married, Joseph was ordained a priest in December of 1583.

In his first years as a priest, Joseph received many administrative responsibilities by the bishops and was on his way to becoming what many in clerical life call a "ladder-climber."

In 1592, when he was 35 years old, he moved to Rome and gave up the money he had as a result of his various clerical positions. With his friend, the great nurse-priest St. Camillus de Lellis, he helped nurse plague victims in 1595.

While in Rome, Joseph began to develop a special sympathy for poor boys. Because nobody would give them an education, Joseph founded the first free school in Rome with the help of some other priests. Later, he founded other schools. By 1602 he had 700 students, and by 1612 he had over 1,200 students. The priests who were helping him lived in a quasi-community, the nucleus of what would eventually become the Piarist Order.

When Fr. Joseph was 65 years old, a priest named Mario Sozzi began a crusade to turn members of the Order against Fr. Joseph. Fr. Sozzi claimed Fr. Joseph was senile and incompetent. Because Fr. Sozzi had many influential friends, Fr. Joseph suffered one humiliation after another at the hands of Sozzi and the leaders that came after him.

Through all of his trials and tribulations, Fr. Joseph suffered with heroic patience and fortitude. He said, "The Lord gave, the Lord hath taken away. Blessed be the name of the Lord." In 1728, Cardinal Lambertini (later Pope Benedict XIV) referred to Joseph as "a perpetual miracle of fortitude and another Job."

Joseph died in Rome on August 25, 1648. He was beatified in 1748 and canonized in 1767. In 1948, Pope Pius XII made him one of the patron saints of Christian schools. His feast day is August 25th.

The life of St. Joseph Calasanz is quite amazing for many reasons. Here are at just three of them.

First, Joseph heard the call of God to be a priest, and answered this call. Like countless people before him, he did this even though there were forces trying to convince him it was a bad idea. In Joseph's case, it was his father who tried to convince him to get married. Joseph, with clarity of vision, knew that God's call trumped his father's wishes.

Second, there may always be enemies lurking when we serve the Lord. When studying the lives of saints, for example, we notice there are many who suffered slings and arrows from people who were jealous of them or who resented them for one reason or another. But that is expected, for Jesus said, "Blessed are they who are persecuted for the sake of righteousness, for theirs is the kingdom of heaven" (Matthew 5: 10).

And third, the life of St. Joseph Calasanz is an awesome example of bearing pain joyfully and patiently. Cardinal Lambertini certainly had it right when he compared St. Joseph to Job. There are so many people in the world who suffer physically, emotionally, and/or spiritually, and they are always in need of solid role models. I especially think of powerless people who suffer from prejudice and discrimination on a daily basis who need models like St. Joseph Calasanz.

As we continue our life journeys this week, it would be a good idea to reflect on our own call from God. How have we been called to help build the kingdom of God here on earth? How have we responded? How do we handle the challenges of our own vocations?

That is the good news I have for you on this Third Sunday in Ordinary Time.

Story source: "St. Joseph Calasanz," in *Butler's Lives of the Saints: New Full Edition*, Reviewed by John Cumming. The Liturgical Press/ Burns & Oates, 1998, pp. 246-248.

Chapter 27

4th Sunday in Ordinary Time - B
Harden Not Your Hearts

Scripture:

- Deuteronomy 18: 15-20
- Psalm 95: 1-2, 6-7c, 7d-9
- 1 Corinthians 7: 32-35
- Mark 1: 21-28

Today, Catholic Christians celebrate the Fourth Sunday in Ordinary Time.

Frequently when we encounter the Scripture passages of the day, certain themes are readily apparent, themes such as forgiveness, generosity, mercy, or the like. Other times, though, they are not quite so visible on first glance. That is the case today. Today, we must dig and reflect more deeply than usual to find a theme to explore. After such digging and reflecting, I have uncovered today's theme: generosity to those in need.

In the Old Testament reading we have today from Deuteronomy, Moses told the people that "A prophet like me will the Lord, your God, raise up for you from among your own kin; to him you shall listen" (Deuteronomy 18: 15). The Lord agreed with Moses and said, "I will raise up for them a prophet like you from among their kin, and will put my words into his mouth; he shall tell them all that I command him. Whoever will not listen to my words which he speaks in my name, I myself will make him answer for it" (Deuteronomy 18: 18-19).

Christians believe that the prophet that Moses and God were foretelling was Jesus. It is Jesus whom we should follow. In the Psalm selection of today, we read that we are to keep our hearts open to the Lord. Specifically, the psalmist says, "Do not harden your hearts" (Psalm 95: 8). And in St. Paul's First Letter to the Corinthians, we are told to keep our focus firmly on Jesus when he tells the Christians of Corinth to adhere to the Lord without distraction (1 Corinthians 7: 35).

Putting all of this together, we know that God would send a prophet that we identify as Jesus, who would tell us God's will for our lives. Because his teaching is directly from God, we are to keep our hearts open to the message and keep focused on God. We are not to become distracted with the things of the world.

As Christians, we already know what Jesus commanded us to do: to love God, to love our neighbors, and to love ourselves. In particular, when it came to how we are to treat human beings, Jesus was crystal clear in putting his greatest emphasis on the poor. He said, "Amen, I say to you, whatever you did for one of these least brothers of mine, you did for me" (Matthew 25: 40).

The Catholic Church calls this Christian commandment the "preferential option for the poor." That means that though we should love and treat all people with dignity and respect as children of God, we should always give priority to the marginalized of society – the poor, the outcast, the prisoner, the victim of prejudice and discrimination. This is the foundation of Catholic social teaching.

In our parish, we give highest emphasis in following this message of Jesus.. In fact, our motto is "Serving God by Serving Others."

In our parish community, we serve the poor in many ways. Our St. Mary-Tileston Social Outreach Ministry, for example, serves 9,000 poor people every year by providing food, clothes, dishes, pots and pans, bedding, bicycles, furniture, toys, and help with utilities and transportation. Our St. Mary Health Center serves the poor in its two clinics: St. Mary Medical Clinic and St. Mary Dental Clinic. And this year, my top priority is helping more of our Hispanic children to get a Catholic education in our St. Mary School.

To meet our missionary mandate, our parish serves the parish of San Francisco de Asís in Reitoca, F.M., Honduras. That parish, with 87 churches and chapels, has 50,000 parishioners, almost all very poor. In a true missionary spirit, we attempt to help the parish help themselves. In other words, we know that they can do everything we can do. What they lack, however, is money. That we can provide.

In a recent visit to our sister parish, for example, we discovered that the staff of Clínica Santa María started a pharmacy with some of the money our parishioners sent from second collections. The pharmacy has been a big success. With the extra money the pharmacy has generated, the clinic has been able to hire a full-time psychologist, which it desperately needed to meet the needs of the people. Currently, the staff is planning on opening two more pharmacies in the towns of La Libertad and Curarén. The Honduran government, meanwhile, will most likely send one or two physicians free of charge to help the clinic in Reitoca and the new one in La Libertad. This is part of the Honduran government's requirement that all professionals must serve the poor for a year before being able to have a license. We look forward to the day when the health care services of the sister parish are fully self-supporting. That is, of course, the dream of every missionary endeavor: to put ourselves out of business, because the people have the necessary resources to take care of themselves.

Although we are delighted to serve our own parish community and our sister parish, we are also responsible for helping our diocese with its ministries. We do this by contributing each year to the Bishop's Annual Appeal. Unlike parishes, which have weekly collections, a diocese must rely on the generosity of the people in an annual appeal.

Money from the Bishop's Annual Appeal goes to help over thirty essential ministries such as seminarian education, campus ministries, Hispanic ministries, African-American ministries, Catholic Charities, marriage preparation, family counseling, faith formation, Catholic schools, and many more. Without our help, none of these critical ministries would be possible.

And that is the good news I have for you on this Fourth Sunday in Ordinary Time.

Chapter 28

5th Sunday in Ordinary Time - B
Depression & St. Noel

Scripture:

- Job 7: 1-4, 6-7
- Psalm 147: 1-2, 3-4, 5-6
- 1 Corinthians 9: 16-19, 22-23
- Mark 1: 29-39

Today, Catholic Christians celebrate the Fifth Sunday in Ordinary Time.

On this day, we encounter an incredible portrait of a man consumed with depression in the selection from Job. Job says:

> Is not man's life on earth a drudgery? Are not his days those of hirelings? He is a slave who longs for the shade, a hireling who waits for his wages. So I have been assigned months of misery, and troubled nights have been allotted to me. If in bed I say, "When shall I arise?" then the night drags on; I am filled with restlessness until the dawn. My days are swifter than a weaver's shuttle; they come to an end without hope. Remember that my life is like the wind; I shall not see happiness again (Job 7: 1-4, 6-7).

This is truly a beautiful presentation of someone in depression, a state of desolation and despondency.

Sometimes, people think that holy people cannot be depressed because they have such great connections with the Lord. That, however, is often not the case. Even holy people can be depressed, as we see in the life of St. Noel Chabanel.

Noel was born in France in 1613 and grew up in a devout Catholic home. In 1630, Noel followed his brother into the Society of Jesus. In his early years in the Jesuit community, he taught rhetoric in a college. In 1641, he was ordained a priest.

At that time the Society of Jesus was experiencing its golden age in France, growing rapidly and sending missionaries to other lands. Fr. Noel caught the missionary spirit and begged to be allowed to go to New France, which is what people in France called Quebec. In 1643, 30-year old Noel set off to Canada, filled with all of the hopes, dreams, visions and zeal that missionaries have always brought to their first assignment.

Fr. Noel arrived in the new world with his Jesuit companions to work with the Huron Indians. Unfortunately, this was a time when the Iroquois Indians were continually trying to kill the Huron Indians. Fear of danger, though, was just the beginning of Fr. Noel's troubles.

Unlike his fellow Jesuits, Noel discovered that he had absolutely no facility for learning a new language. His experience for learning the language was so bad, in fact, that his superior, Fr. Paul Ragueneau, said, "Once here, even after three, four, five years of study of the Indian language, [Fr. Noel] made such little progress that he could hardly be understood even in the most ordinary conversation. This was no small mortification for a man burning with the desire to convert the Indians. Besides, it was particularly painful, for his memory had always been good, as were his other talents, which was proven by his years of satisfactory teaching of rhetoric in France."

To add to his miserable failure at learning a language, Noel found that absolutely everything about the Huron Indians was disgusting to him. He hated their customs and found their food revolting. All of these factors left Fr. Noel deeply depressed.

Fortunately, however, Noel was aware of his failures and emotions and was honest with himself. So despite his complete distaste for the Huron Indian culture and food, and his lack of language ability, Noel believed that God had called him to be a missionary to these people. Therefore, in front of the Blessed Sacrament on the Feast of Corpus Christi 1647, Fr. Noel made a vow of perpetual stability to the Huron people.

Fr. Noel, in various missions with the Huron Indians, kept himself busy by assisting other, more competent priests in their pastoral work. He worked with great humility and fidelity. In 1649, a Huron apostate killed Fr. Noel out of hatred for the Christian faith. Along with seven other Jesuit martyrs, he was canonized in 1930. This group is often called the "North American Martyrs," although there would one day be many more North American martyrs, notably in Mexico during the Cristero war.

The life of Noel and the reading from Job can teach us many things.

First, sanctity does not prevent one from suffering from depression. Today, depression is seen as a mental health issue, not a moral failure. Sometimes, depression is called "situational," that is, it is most likely caused by the circumstances one finds in life. That, certainly, is seen in Fr. Noel's life. Other times, the root of depression is a biochemical state, which has no apparent situational cause.

Second, frequently people can still meet their adult responsibilities even though suffering from depression. That is what we see in the life of St. Noel. Despite his constant failures in his life as a missionary, he continually served, day after day, by assisting other priests in their work. Sometimes, however, depression can be so debilitating that work is impossible. When that happens, people need to use every ounce of energy just to do the simplest things of daily life, things like getting dressed or eating. Counseling and/or medical therapy are very often effective in helping people who are so distressed.

And third, as Christians, we are called to be sensitive and compassionate for those who suffer depression and other forms of mental distress. We are to avoid giving harsh and meaningless advice such as saying, "Snap out of it!" We would never think of telling someone afflicted with cancer to "snap out of it," and we should not do so with depression.

As we continue our life journeys this week, it might be a good idea to reflect on our own life journeys. Have we been afflicted with depression at various times in our lives? What helped us in these periods? How do we help those around us suffering from depression?

And that is the good news I have for you on this Fifth Sunday in Ordinary Time.

Story sources:

"St. Noel Chabanel" in *Saints and Angels – Catholic Online.*

Ambrosie, Peter, "Noel Chabanel - 1613-1649 – Wyandot Nation of Kansas," www.wyandot.org/chabanel.htm.

Chapter 29

6th Sunday in Ordinary Time - B
Seton & Stigma

Scripture:

- Leviticus 13: 1-2, 44-46
- Psalm 32: 1-2, 5, 11
- 1 Corinthians 10: 31 – 11: 1
- Mark 1: 40-45

Today, Catholic Christians celebrate the Sixth Sunday in Ordinary Time.

On this day, we hear a very interesting message from the Book of Leviticus, one of the books of the Torah, the first five books of the Old Testament. In this passage, we hear how someone that had a sore that could indicate leprosy should be brought to the priest. If the priest determined that such persons had leprosy, they had to isolate themselves from other people. If they should encounter other people, they must call out that they are unclean so that others wouldn't come in contact with them. The idea was to protect healthy people from catching the disease of leprosy, which was incurable in those days. The other reason was that people thought disease was caused by sin in those days, so isolating and shunning others was a way of showing moral superiority.

The custom of treating others as lepers has always been part of human society. The process of treating others as "contaminated" or "damaged" is called stigmatization. A *stigma* is a characteristic that the majority of society sees as discrediting. Examples of stigmata include bodily disfigurements especially of the face, being from a low caste, or having a criminal label. Sometimes one's religious identity can even be a stigma. That is exactly what we see in the life of St. Elizabeth Ann Seton.

Elizabeth Ann Seton was born in 1774 in New York City, two years before the United States of America declared itself independent from England. Her parents were Episcopalians and members of high society.

When she was three years old, her mother died. Her father, Dr. Richard Bailey, did his best to raise Elizabeth. He influenced her greatly to be an avid reader, and Elizabeth developed a special love of religious and historical subjects. She especially loved reading the Bible.

When she was 19 years old in 1794, Elizabeth married William Seton and with him had five children. In these early years of her marriage, Elizabeth formed a close friendship with her sister-in-law, Rebecca. The two of them did so much mission work for the poor of the city, that people began calling them the "Protestant Sisters of Charity."

Unfortunately, William's firm went bankrupt around 1802, and at about the same time he developed tuberculosis. On the advice of his physicians, he took his family to Italy for the benefits of a warmer climate. In 1803 he died, leaving Elizabeth to raise five children by herself. Fortunately, however, she had friends in Italy who supported her.

While she was in Italy, Elizabeth fell in love with Catholic Christianity. The more she explored, the more she was convinced that this was the church Christ had founded. She especially loved the Eucharist and other sacraments.

On Ash Wednesday of 1805, Elizabeth became a Catholic, and shortly afterward she came back to the United States.

Unfortunately for her, being a Catholic Christian was a great stigma in New York in those days. And because her family and friends in the United States were very anti-Catholic, they ostracized her and her children. Furthermore, when she tried to establish a school for boys in the suburbs of New York with a Catholic friend and his wife, the school was forced to close, as people believe it was simply a front to proselytize others to the Catholic faith. And when her sister-in-law Cecilia Seton expressed her desire to become a Catholic, the New York legislature threatened to expel Elizabeth from the state of New York.

Elizabeth, despite these adverse consequences, remained faithful to her new faith. In fact, she jumped into it with great fervor. While raising her five children, she opened a school for girls in Baltimore on the feast of Corpus Christi, 1808.

In the village of Emmitsburg, Maryland, Elizabeth received a gift of a farm, which she turned into an institution to teach poor children. Other women joined her and, despite great poverty and harsh conditions, the institution flourished. This community grew into a religious order called the Sisters of Charity of St. Joseph. In 1813, Elizabeth with 18 other women made their vows as Religious Sisters.

Mother Seton, as she was known in her community, died in Emmitsburg on January 4, 1821. She was canonized on September 14, 1975, becoming the first saint born in the United States. Her feast day is January 4th.

The life of St. Elizabeth gives us a glimpse into the power of a stigma, a discrediting characteristic that a person possesses. In her case, it was her Catholic faith. Her life shows that what makes a characteristic a stigma is not the individual or the characteristic itself. Rather, it is the society that labels it as such. Thus, to get rid of a stigma, one must change the society, not the individual characteristic.

St. Elizabeth's life also shows how one can rise above hate and discrimination with God's help. Despite being shunned by family and friends, Elizabeth simply became stronger. After all, steel becomes stronger when tempered with fire.

You and I, as Catholic Christians, have a moral obligation to show special compassion and sensitivity toward those bearing a stigma, no matter what kind. We do this because Jesus has commanded us to do so when he gave us the triple love command.

As we continue our life journeys this week, it would be a good idea to reflect on our own lives. How do we treat others who carry a stigma? How could we be more sensitive and loving toward them?

And that is the good news I have for you on this Sixth Sunday in Ordinary Time.

Story source:

Bartles, F.K., "Elizabeth Ann Seton: The First American-Born Saint," *Catholic Online* (www.catholic.org), January 4, 2012.

Chapter 30

7th Sunday in Ordinary Time - B
August's Giving

Scripture:

- Isaiah 43: 18-19, 21-22, 24b-25
- Psalm 41: 2-3, 4-5, 13-14
- 2 Corinthians 1: 18-22
- Mark 2: 1-12

Today, Catholic Christians celebrate the Seventh Sunday in Ordinary Time.

On this day, we read in the psalm about how important it is to be concerned for the poor. Specifically, we read:

> "Blessed is he who has concern for the poor.
>   In time of trouble, the Lord will rescue him.
> The Lord will guard him, give him life
>   and make him blessed in the land,
>   not give him up to the will of his foes.
> The Lord will help him on his bed of pain,
>   you will bring him back from sickness to health"
> (Psalm 41: 2-4).

This psalm passage is not unique, for all throughout the Old and New Testaments we read how special the poor are in the heart of God.

Before looking at a few principles pertaining to caring for the poor, however, let's look at the following story about a preacher who showed how to be generous, and as a result, was showered with many blessings.

In the latter part of the 17th century, a German preacher named August Hermann Francke founded an orphanage to care for the homeless children of Halle.

One day, a destitute Christian widow came to his door begging for a ducat – a gold coin. Unfortunately, however, Rev. Francke desperately needed funds to carry on his own work. When he told the woman that he was unable to give her any money, she began to weep. Moved by her tears, August asked her to wait while he went to his room to pray for divine guidance.

After his prayer, August felt that the Holy Spirit was directing him to give the woman some money. Therefore, trusting that somehow God would take care of his needs, August gave the woman some money.

Two mornings later, he found a thank you letter from the widow whom he had helped. The widow explained that because of his generosity, she had asked the Lord to shower his orphanage with gifts. That same day, August received twelve ducats from a wealthy woman and two more from a friend in Sweden.

Rev. Francke was amazed at his good fortune, but he soon learned that the gift of fourteen ducats was nothing compared to what he would soon receive. A short while later, he learned that his orphanage had inherited 500 ducats from the estate of Prince Lodewyk Van Wurtenburg. When he heard this good news, Rev. Francke wept with joy and gratitude. He learned that generosity begets generosity, for by helping the needy widow, God helped him and his projects.

From this beautiful story and from the psalm we have today, we can learn many things. Here are just three.

First, giving to the poor is a commandment, not only in the New Testament, but also in the Old Testament. Therefore, we are obligated to care for the poor because that is what God wants us to do. God's commands to us are always quite sufficient a reason for us to do something.

Sometimes, people falsely believe that if a command of God is not in the Hebrew "Ten Commandments," then it is not really a "commandment." That is not true. "Forgive your enemy" (Matthew 5: 44) and "Give drink to the thirsty" (Matthew 25: 35) are commandments just as "real" as "Honor thy father and thy mother" (Exodus 20: 12). Christians especially should know this. Unfortunately, though, Christians often ignore Jesus' commandments because they have no intention of following them, commandments such as "forgive your enemies."

Second, when we give to the poor we give to Christ, who lives in every human being. Jesus taught that, "Amen, I say to you, whatever you did for one of these least brothers of mine, you did for me" (Matthew 25: 40). Mother Teresa of Calcutta was a most spectacular example of recognizing Christ in even the most forgotten human beings – people whom nobody wanted or respected, dying on the streets of Calcutta.

And third, when we give to the poor, we will receive a reward. That is what we read in the psalm of today. We also read this promise in many other places of the Scriptures. In the Gospel of Luke, for example, we read, "Give and gifts will be given to you; a good measure, packed together, shaken down, and overflowing, will be poured into your lap. For the measure with which you measure will in return be measured out to you" (Luke 6: 38).

Though Jesus asks us to give alms, he warns us that if we give for glory, we will not receive a reward. Specifically, he says, "When you give alms, do not blow a trumpet before you, as the hypocrites do in the synagogues and in the streets to win the praise of others. Amen, I say to you, they have received their reward" (Matthew 6: 2).

As we continue our life journeys this week, it would be a good idea to reflect on our own lives. How do we give to the poor? How has God blessed our generosity? Do we give with humility?

And that is the good news I have for you on this Seventh Sunday in Ordinary Time.

Story source: The story of August H. Francke is from *Sermon Illustrations*, World Wide Web, August 20, 2015.

Chapter 31

8th Sunday in Ordinary Time - B
It Led to Ben-Hur

Scripture:

- Hosea 2: 16b, 17b, 21-22
- Psalm 103: 1-2, 3-4, 8 & 10, 12-13
- 2 Corinthians 3: 1b-6
- Mark 2: 18-22

Today, Catholic Christians celebrate the Eighth Sunday in Ordinary Time.

On this day, we read about the concept of growth and change. In partial answer to why the disciples of John fasted while the disciples of Jesus did not, Jesus replied, "No one sews a piece of unshrunken cloth on an old cloak. If he does, its fullness pulls away, the new from the old, and the tear gets worse. Likewise, no one pours new wine into old wineskins. Otherwise, the wine will burst the skins, and both the wine and the skins are ruined. Rather, new wine is poured into fresh wineskins" (Mark 2: 21-22).

This passage is just as important to us today as it was in the time of Jesus, for it teaches us many important things about life. But before exploring some of these points, let's look at the story of a man who discovered that he had to change his life to be fulfilled.

Sometime in the nineteenth century, two American men were riding on a train. Both of the men were famous for making fun of Christianity. On this particular day, one of the men said to the other, "People are still enamored of Christianity and this man Jesus Christ. You are a writer. Why don't you write a book exposing Jesus for the fraud that he is?" The man who made the suggestion of Colonel Robert Ingersoll, and his companion was General Lew Wallace.

General Wallace, who lived from 1827-1905, was a very famous military figure in the Mexican-American War and the Civil War, and was later the Governor of the New Mexico Territory of the United States. Though he was a lawyer by education, law did not give him much pleasure, so he turned to his passion – writing books.

Now General Wallace was a very thorough man. He wanted to be sure that what he wrote was accurate. Therefore, he began to do extensive research on a book to expose Jesus as a fraud. To do that, however, he first had to read and study the Bible and do some background reading.

He came to the conclusion, however, that reading and studying were not enough. He decided he had to go to the Holy Land. Now, for the first time, he began to talk with simple people who had great faith. Before this time, he had only spoken to sophisticated university scholars and writers.

By the time he was done with his study, General Wallace wrote his most famous book, *Ben-Hur: A Tale of the Christ.* Many people regard the novel, first published in 1880, as the most influential Christian book of the nineteenth century. Pope Leo XIII blessed the book, the first work of fiction ever receiving such an honor.

In 1959, MGM made *Ben-Hur* into a movie, and in 1960, it won eleven Academy Awards.

One of the most important lines in the book is when a centurion says, "Truly, this is the Son of God."

Lew Wallace led a most interesting and fulfilling life that ties in beautifully with today's Gospel selection from St. Mark. Though we could explore many ideas gleaned from this passage, here are just three.

First, life is not static: it is always changing. We cannot grow without change. Sometimes, people forget that. They fear change, for that often means entering into previously unexplored territories.

Fortunately, there are some questions that can stimulate growth in our lives. How are our virtues expanding? What kinds of new adventures have we always wanted to take but never got around to? What kinds of dreams do we hold, and how can we achieve them? What kinds of hobbies or other interests can we develop? How are we developing our minds? How are we developing our bodies? What kinds of spiritual exercises could we be doing to flex our "spiritual muscles?"

Second, the Holy Spirit leads us to change and grow in a wide variety of ways. In the case of General Wallace, the Spirit led him to become a Christian through his love of research and writing. Often, the Spirit leads us to change through contact with family, friends, and coworkers. At other times, the Spirit leads us through writers. Very many saints' lives were dramatically changed through reading books. Sometimes the Spirit touches our hearts through preachers and other speakers. And the most powerful and direct way the Spirit leads us is by planting strong desires deep in our hearts. For example, people often choose a profession based on a strong attraction.

And third, what works perfectly at one point in our lives may not be so good at another point in our lives. Today, many people of the world are living longer and longer lives. Much more than in the distant past, people find themselves in more than one profession or vocation. In Catholic seminaries today, for example, we see many men who had other careers before entering the seminary. I know many seminarians and priests who are also nurses, lawyers, engineers, writers, sociologists, musicians, and teachers. And many people find their greatest joys and creative energies in retirement. Thus, we need to always be ready to travel on new paths.

As we continue our life journeys this week, it would be a good idea to reflect on our own lives. How are we growing mentally, physically, and spiritually? How can we do better?

And that is the good news I have for you on this Eighth Sunday in Ordinary Time.

Story source: Anonymous, "The Agnostics," in William J. Bausch, *A World of Stories for Preachers and Teachers*, Mystic, Connecticut, Twenty-Third Publications, 1998, #132, pp. 279-280.

Chapter 32

9th Sunday in Ordinary Time - B
The List

Scripture:

- Deuteronomy 5: 12-15
- Psalm 81: 3-4, 5-6ab, 6c-8a, 10-11b
- 2 Corinthians 4: 6-11
- Mark 2: 23 – 3: 6

Today, Catholic Christians celebrate the Ninth Sunday in Ordinary Time.

On this day, we read an incredibly important passage from the Gospel of Mark about how we are to distinguish the "spirit" of the law from the "letter" of the law.

In this passage, the Pharisees were criticizing Jesus' disciples because they were picking grain to eat as they passed through wheat fields on the Sabbath. The Pharisees considered this to be "work," and they pointed out to Jesus that God does not want people to work on the Sabbath.

Jesus gave the Pharisees an example from the Old Testament scriptures showing how even King David and his companions gathered food on the Sabbath. Then, Jesus said to the Pharisees, "The Sabbath was made for man, not man for the Sabbath" (Mark 2: 27). And to put his teaching into action, he asked a man with a withered hand to come to him. Then, he asked the Pharisees, "Is it lawful to do good on the Sabbath rather than to do evil, to save life rather than to destroy it?" (Mark 3: 4). When the Pharisees remained silent, Jesus cured the man on the Sabbath.

This passage contains important principles that are just as important today as they were in the time of Jesus. But before looking at a few of them, let's look at a story attributed to Kara Powell from Ben Patterson's book, *Serving God*.

There was once a woman who was married to a perfectionistic man. No matter what his wife did for him, he was never satisfied. At the beginning of every day, the man would make out a list of chores for his wife. Then, at the end of each day, he would scrutinize the list to see if she had done everything. Even though she always did her best, it was never enough for her husband. He never gave her a compliment. The closest thing to a compliment was a grunt if she had finished everything on the list.

Needless to say, the woman came to hate her husband. It was not surprising, then, that when he dropped dead unexpectedly one day, the woman was not at all sad. In fact, she was relieved.

Within a year of her husband's death, the woman met a warm and loving man who was everything her first husband was not. They fell in love with each other and were married. As a couple, they lived a very joyful life.

One afternoon, as the woman was cleaning out boxes in the attic, she came across a crumpled piece of paper. When she opened it up, she discovered that it was one of the old chore lists written by her first husband. She could not help reading it again. To her shock and amazement, she discovered that without even thinking about it, she was now doing the very same tasks for her current husband. Her current husband had never asked her to do any of those things, but now she enjoyed doing them. She enjoyed doing them because she loved her new husband, and doing things for him was one of the ways she was able to express that love in a concrete way.

This is a wonderful story for today, because it reminds us of how we are to approach the guidelines God has given us. Here are just three things we can glean from today's scripture passage from St. Mark.

First, we must always be careful not to focus exclusively on the letter of the law, for that can lead us to make the law, itself, an idol. Certain people are more prone to doing this than others. Some are so rigid in their thinking that they almost worship laws. Through its 2,000-year history, the Catholic Church has had many people called "legalists" and "rigorists." Such people usually have very rigid personalities and tend to see the world in absolutes. They view the world in terms of black and white, good and evil. They cannot see shades of grey. Often, such people see the Church itself as a house of cards, which can collapse if just one card is taken away. For them, change of any kind is terrifying, for it flies in the face of their "absolutist" thinking.

Second, we need to look at why a law or rule was made. For Catholic Christians, laws are guides to behavior. They are to help us walk on our life journeys with as much gracefulness as possible. They are not meant to be roadblocks designed to prevent us from growing and flourishing.

When we know why a law was made in the first place, we are in a better position to know when to ignore it. For example, when I was a young R.N., there was a rule in the hospital that all visitors had to be out by 8 p.m. The rationale was that patients needed adequate rest so they could heal. That made perfect sense. However, nurses discovered that such a rule, when put into practice, often did the opposite of what it was supposed to do. On pediatric wards, for example, little children would often become hysterical when their parents left. This would, of course, prevent them from getting adequate rest. Based on such experiences, such rules were eventually relaxed. In fact, parents were eventually encouraged to stay the whole night!

And third, as Catholic Christians, we believe in a "hierarchy" of values, rules, etc. In other words, a proscription against killing is of greater value than a proscription against stealing. Likewise, virtues are in a hierarchy, with charity or love at the very top. Thus, we need to consider what law, rule, or virtue "trumps" another.

As we continue our life journeys this week, it would be a good idea to reflect on how we see law. Do we distinguish between the spirit and letter of the law?

And that is the good news I have for you on this Ninth Sunday in Ordinary Time.

Story source: Kara Powell, "The List" in Wayne Rice (Ed.), *Hot Illustrations for Youth Talks*. Grand Rapids, Michigan, Youth Specialties/Zondervan, 2001, pp. 60-61.

Chapter 33

10th Sunday in Ordinary Time - B
The Three Trees

Scripture:

- Genesis 3: 9-15
- Psalm 130: 1-2, 3-4, 5-6ab & 7a, 7b-8
- 2 Corinthians 4: 13 – 5: 1
- Mark 3: 20-35

Today, Catholic Christians celebrate the Tenth Sunday in Ordinary Time.

On this day, we read a passage from St. Paul's second letter to the Corinthians about how fleeting life is and how wonderful the next life will be. This passage is often chosen as a funeral reading.

Today, I focus on this part of Paul's letter: "Therefore, we are not discouraged; rather, although our outer self is wasting away, our inner self is being renewed day by day. For this momentary light affliction is producing for us an eternal weight of glory beyond all comparison, as we look not to what is seen but to what is unseen; for what is seen is transitory, but what is unseen is eternal. For we know that if our earthly dwelling, a tent, should be destroyed, we have a building from God, a dwelling not made with hands, eternal in heaven" (2 Corinthians 4: 16 – 5: 1).

Before examining a few of the points we can glean from this important passage, let's look at an old folktale that shows what we desire is often so much less than what we will ultimately receive. Amelia Elwell Hunt named the story "The Three Trees."

There once were three little trees growing on a mountaintop. They loved dreaming of what they would be when they grew up.

The first little tree wanted to become a treasure chest, holding beautiful gold and diamonds and other precious stones.

The second little tree, as it looked at the small stream trickling by on its way to the ocean, decided it wanted to become a mighty ship carrying kings and other important people.

The third little tree gazed at the valley below. It decided that it did not want to leave the mountain at all. Instead, it wanted to grow to be the tallest tree on the mountain. Then, people would look up to it and raise their eyes to heaven and think of God.

Many years passed, and the trees flourished and grew tall and strong. Soon, it was time for them to be harvested.

The first tree, that wanted to be a magnificent treasure chest, was devastated to learn it would become a simple manger for hungry farm animals. The second tree, that wanted to be a beautiful ship, was fashioned into a simple fishing boat. And the third tree, that wanted to remain living on the mountain as a symbol of glory to God, was cut down and made into wooden beams for Roman soldiers to use to execute criminals.

Many days passed, and the trees lost their dreams. But then one night, a young woman in Bethlehem placed her little baby into the manger. Thus, the first tree became the first bed for the baby Jesus.

Some years passed, and the second tree realized that it, too, was now holding the greatest treasure in the world. One night, when there was a huge storm, one of the men in the boat – a man named Jesus - commanded the wind and storm to be silent, and they did. The tree, now a fishing boat, was overwhelmed at the idea that it was carrying the savior of the world.

Finally, one Friday morning, the third tree was startled to discover that its beams were being used to crucify Jesus. The tree felt ugly and abused. It felt ashamed that instead of being used to glorify God, it had become an agent of death. However, on Sunday morning, when the sun rose, so did Jesus. Now, every time people thought of the third tree, they would think of God. That was better than being the tallest tree in the world.

Though all of the trees had had dreams, none of them came true in the way they had imagined. Rather, the outcomes became much, much more than their dreams.

That is what, in effect, St. Paul was saying. Keep our eyes not on this life, but on the next. Here are just three things we can glean from St. Paul's Second Letter to the Corinthians.

First, like all major world religions, Christianity deals with the reality that life on this planet is transitory, fleeting. Paul, who suffered more in his life than most of us will ever suffer, always remembered that our earthly suffering was nothing compared to the joys that will come in the afterlife. This theme is seen especially in the songs and stories of people whose suffering on this earth is great.

Second, because this life is transitory, and because we need to prepare ourselves for the next life, it is good to be prepared. We remain prepared in three ways: by praying to God each day; by living our vocations as best we can for the greater honor and glory of God; and by living the triple-love command of Jesus each and every day.

And third, we need to continually keep in mind that the best is yet to come. Many people have compared heaven to the "dessert" of our existence. Because the best is yet to come, we should have our priorities straight. We should always be asking ourselves how our actions are demonstrating our belief in God and heaven. For example, some people are so attached to living in this world, that they go to extraordinary lengths to avoid earthly death. It is as if they do not believe that the "best is yet to come."

As we continue our life journeys this week, it would be a good idea to reflect on our own lives. Are our priorities straight? Are we prepared for the afterlife?

And that is the good news I have for you on this Ninth Sunday in Ordinary Time.

Story source: Angela Elwell Hunt, "The Three Trees: A Traditional Folktale," David C. Cook, Publisher, 1989.

Chapter 34

11th Sunday in Ordinary Time - B
The Noodle Priest

Scripture:

- Ezekiel 17: 22-24
- Psalm 92: 2-3, 13-14, 15-16
- 2 Corinthians 5: 6-10
- Mark 4: 26-34

Today, Catholic Christians celebrate the Eleventh Sunday in Ordinary Time.

On this day, we hear Jesus tell two parables from the world of agriculture to give the disciples an idea of what the "kingdom of God" is like. In the second parable, Jesus compares the kingdom of God to a mustard seed. He says, "It is like a mustard seed that, when it is sown in the ground, is the smallest of all the seeds on the earth. But once it is sown, it springs up and becomes the largest of plants and puts forth large branches, so that the birds of the sky can dwell in its shade" (Mark 4: 31-32).

This parable can teach us many principles, but first, let's look at a story of how one American man planted seeds that served millions.

The story begins in China in the middle of the twentieth century. A man named Mao Zedong brought Communism to China. When that happened, many Christian missionaries were imprisoned, tortured, killed, or expelled from the country.

The Maryknoll Fathers, Brothers, and Sisters were among those who suffered at the hands of the Communists. And some of the missionaries fled to Hong Kong, which at that time was an island colony of Great Britain.

In just a couple of years after 1949, refugees fleeing from China made their way to Hong Kong. Soon, the island's population grew from 500,000 people to more than two-and-a-half million people. Some people described the Hong Kong of those days as the "largest refugee camp" in the entire world.

One of the priests who found his way to Hong Kong from China was a Maryknoll missionary priest named John Romaniello.

John was born in 1900 in Avigliana, Italy. When he was 9 years old, his parents moved the family to New Rochelle, New York to begin a new life.

In 1928, John graduated from Catholic University in Washington, D.C. and was ordained a Maryknoll priest. Though he wrote many books, Msgr. John – as he came to be known –is perhaps best known for his novel called *Bird of Sorrow* that is based on his many years in China.

Fr. John was sent to work in China, the land where Maryknoll missionaries first began their mission work. There, he labored in various capacities until the Communists captured and expelled him in 1948

After his expulsion from China, Msgr. John returned to the United States to obtain a master's degree from Yale University in 1954 while teaching at Maryknoll Seminary in New York. After serving for two years in Rome, Msgr. John went to work in Hong Kong until 1971.

It was there that John became famous throughout the world as "The Noodle Priest of Hong Kong."

Refugees poured into Hong Kong from China, many of them poor and hungry. Maryknoll missionaries, like others, worked constantly to help the refugees help themselves.

One day, while Msgr. John was walking around, he noticed something very strange. He saw many poor people lining up at a store holding bags of wheat flour in their hands. When it was their turn, they would turn over their bags of wheat flour to the storeowner, who would make their flour into noodles. One pound of flour would become one pound of noodles.

Msgr. John learned that the flour had come from the United States' program called Food for Peace. This program provided flour, cornmeal and powdered milk. Unfortunately, the Chinese people did not eat bread.

Msgr. John, with American ingenuity and a little money, had an idea. He quickly obtained a dozen electric noodle machines to turn flour into noodles. In time, he established noodle factories throughout Hong Kong, allowing poor refugees to eat what they liked – pasta. Msgr. John said that giving pasta to the Chinese immigrants was simply a matter of reciprocity. He said, "For centuries, my Italian forebears enjoyed spaghetti, the food brought back from China by Marco Polo. I brought noodles to the Chinese at the rate of millions of pounds a year."

In time, Msgr. John Romaniello came to be known as "The Noodle Priest of Hong Kong" and was even a guest on the old television show called *What's My Line?* He died of cancer at the age of 85 on October 23, 1985.

From the parable of the mustard seed and Msgr. Romaniello's life, we can learn many things. Here are just three.

First, God is the sower who sends seeds to us. The seeds we receive can be dreams, ideas, values, knowledge, and other things we often see as "intangibles."

Second, we are the soil in which God plants the seeds. And just as rich soil helps plants thrive better than poor soil, the richer we are in ambition, knowledge and desire to make this a better world, the more we are able to produce.

And third, to make the seeds God sends us grow, we must put our dreams and visions and plans into action. That is what we see in the life of The Noodle Priest. If he didn't begin setting up noodle factories, all of his knowledge and money would have accomplished little. But because he did get busy, millions were able to eat.

As we continue our life journeys this week, it would be a good idea to reflect on our own lives. What kind of seeds has God sown in our hearts? How are we growing them?

And that is the good news I have for you on this Eleventh Sunday in Ordinary Time.

Story sources:

- Maryknoll's Monsignor John Romaniello, Famed Hong Kong 'Noodle Priest' Dies, October 23, 1985 – Hong Kong, WWW.
- "The Noodle Priest," CRS in the 1950s, WWW.
- "Noodle Priest of Hong Kong" Is Dead at 85, *Times Wire Service,* October 25, 1985, WWW.

Chapter 35

12th Sunday in Ordinary Time - B
The Storm

Scripture:

- Job 38: 1, 8-11
- Psalm 107: 23-24, 25-26, 28-29, 30-31
- 2 Corinthians 5: 14-17
- Mark 4: 35-41

1

Today, Catholic Christians celebrate the Twelfth Sunday in Ordinary Time.

On this day, we read the interesting story of Jesus and his disciples caught in a storm on the sea. While Jesus was fast asleep on a pillow, the disciples were terrified as a violent squall made the waves toss the boat around.

The disciples, terrified, woke Jesus up and said, "Teacher, do you not care that we are perishing?" (Mark 4: 38) Jesus responded by calmly ordering the wind to be quiet. Suddenly, a great calm came over the sea. Needless to say, the disciples were astonished and said to one another, "Who then is this whom even wind and sea obey?" (Mark 4: 41).

This story can teach us many things. But before we explore a few of these things, let's first look at a story called "The Storm."

There was once a pastor whose ministry took him all over the country. One evening, as he was on a long flight, the pilot turned on the "Fasten Seat Belts" sign. A short time later, a flight attendant calmly announced, "We will not be serving any beverages at this time because we are experiencing a little turbulence. Please be sure your seat belt is fastened."

The pastor looked around the aircraft, and he noticed that many of the people were looking a bit apprehensive. A short while later, one of the flight attendants announced that they would not be able to serve the dinner they had been planning to serve because of turbulence ahead.

A few minutes later, a storm came full force. The passengers heard ominous cracks of thunder even over the roar of the engines. Lightning bolts lit up the darkened skies. In a moment, the plane became like a cork tossed around on waves of a stormy ocean. One minute, the airplane was lifted on powerful currents of air, and the next minute, it dropped as though it were going to crash.

By now, everyone on the plane was beginning to panic, including the pastor. Some of the people were praying. Some were crying. The future seemed very ominous, and many were wondering if they would live through the storm.

As the pastor looked around the plane at the alarmed passengers, he was astonished see a little girl who acted as though the storm didn't even exist. She had her feet tucked beneath her as she sat. She was calmly reading a book as the plane bobbed up and down on the fierce air currents. Sometimes, she would close her eyes, and then she would read again. Sometimes she would straighten her legs. Her little world was totally peaceful.

The pastor was amazed at this child. How could she be so calm while all the adults in the airplane were frightened to death? He was determined to seek her out when, and if, the plane landed safely.

Fortunately for the pastor and all of the other passengers, the plane did land safely. The pastor sought out the little girl and asked her why she had not been afraid in the storm.

She replied simply, "Sir, my daddy is the pilot, and he is taking me home."

The pastor was amazed at the child's simplicity and the great faith she put in her father and his care for her. Needless to say, the pastor could not help but reflect on this experience, and he used it more than once in homilies.

You and I can learn much from the Scripture story of Jesus sleeping in the storm and the little girl in the story. Here are just three of them.

First, everyone experience storms in their lives. These storms are troubles we experience in various life realms, realms such as physical health, spirituality, finances, work, school, mental health, and others.

In our community, as in all communities, many of our members suffer from addictions. Others suffer from depression and grief. Others are battling conditions such as cancer and heart conditions. Others are drowning in credit card debt and worried about how they're going to pay basic bills.

One thing I have learned in life – but that I tend to forget from time to time – is that everyone has problems. Everyone experiences storms in life.

Second, like the pilot in the story, our Father is in charge. We so often forget that basic fact. We imagine that we must control every little thing in our environment.

And third, like the little girl in the story, we are to put our faith in the pilot of our lives – God. We put our faith in God not only when we acknowledge God and his ultimate control over the universe, but also when we become active participants in his rule. Although we know God is in charge, we also know that we have to do our part to live responsible lives.

In Pope Francis' latest encyclical, *Laudato Si: On the Care of Our Common Home,* for example, the pope admonishes all human beings to be active participants in serving the poor of the world and caring for our planet. We can't sit back and assume that God is going to feed the hungry and clean up the planet on his own. After all, as Jesus told humanity before his ascension into heaven, we are now his eyes and ears and hands and feet and mouth. We are his body, and as his body, we are to get busy and continue his work. All of this is what "having faith" means.

As we continue our life journeys this week, it would be a good idea to reflect on the storms of our lives and how we demonstrate our trust that God will care for us.

And that is the good news I have for you on this Twelfth Sunday in Ordinary Time.

Story source: Anonymous, "The Storm," on *2 Jesus: Inspiring Stories*, World Wide Web.

Chapter 36

13th Sunday in Ordinary Time - B
The Message

Scripture:

- Wisdom 1: 13-15; 2: 23-24
- Psalm 30: 2 & 4, 5-6, 11 & 12a & 13b
- 2 Corinthians 8: 7, 9, 13-15
- Mark 5: 21-43

Today, Catholic Christians celebrate the Thirteenth Sunday in Ordinary Time.

On this day, we encounter Jesus healing a woman and a girl in the Gospel of Mark (Mark 5: 21-43). In the first instance, he healed a woman who had been suffering from bleeding for twelve years, and in the second instance, he raised a synagogue official's daughter from the dead.

Stories such as these are important in understanding our Catholic Christian faith, because from the earliest days of the Church, Catholic Christians have put a heavy emphasis on caring for the sick.

In the United States, for example, our Catholic ancestors made it a point to establish Catholic hospitals, clinics, and nursing centers as they built parishes and schools. When I lived in Montana and in Washington State, for example, I was amazed at the number of Catholic hospitals. Many of them dated back almost a century.

Healing usually refers to restoring someone to health or curing a malady with which a person suffers. Often, healing is associated with the field of medicine. Caring for the sick, on the other hand, refers to the treatment of human responses to actual or potential illnesses. Caring, in addition to healing, is more associated with nursing.

But whether we talk about healing the sick or caring for the sick, we need to always keep in mind that "sickness" is not just something that happens to the body. It can happen to the mind and spirit. If we forget that, we are likely to miss many opportunities to be Christ for others. That point is what we might initially miss in the following story called "The Message."

There was once a young man named Thomas who was an only child. His father had died when Thomas was much younger. He loved his mother – Joyce - very much, and he rejoiced with her when she battled cancer and was cancer-free for five years.

One day, his mother had exploratory surgery. Following the procedure, the surgeon told Thomas that Joyce's cancer had returned and that there was nothing more he could do. He said she only had three months to live.

After Joyce had spent a few days in the hospital, it became obvious to Thomas that the surgeon had not told her the devastating news. Therefore, he was the one who had to tell her. Though mother and son had always been close, the deeply personal conversation brought them even closer.

After bringing his mother home from the hospital, Thomas returned to his job as a hairstylist in New York. Shortly after, however, he returned to his mother's home to spend a month with her. During that month, mother and son enjoyed each other's company, talking about everything – politics, philosophy, current events, and religion. Though Joyce loved her son immensely, she was very sad that Thomas was an agnostic, a person who doubts the existence of God. For Thomas, when you're dead, you're dead. That's the end of the story, in his mind.

That saddened Joyce very much, for she had always been a very religious person. As a young woman, she had even been in a convent for two years as a Religious Sister.

After a month, Thomas had to return to his job in New York. But before he left, his mother gave him a special gift – a beautiful cross that was one of the most precious possessions that she had received while a Sister.

Within a month, Thomas got the call he had been dreading: his mother was dying and he should come quickly.

Unfortunately, his mother died while Thomas was in flight from New York. After the funeral, though he mourned, he was deeply glad that they had had a special month together.

The big part of the story, however, came three months after Joyce's death. A prominent businesswoman, who was a client of Thomas, came to get her hair done. She was the type of person who treated others with a reserved air of cool politeness. She had never shared much with Thomas, so he was surprised that one day she let it slip that she had cancer.

On this day, the woman said, "Thomas, I hesitate to tell you this because I know it is going to sound very strange. I have a strong feeling that I'm supposed to tell you that Anita?...Marie?...Mary?...Anita Mary is okay. She said to tell you everything is all right."

Thomas was astonished. Though his mother's given name was Joyce, in Religious life she was known as Sr. Anita Mary – the name that had been inscribed on the back of the cross she had given him. No one knew this fact except Thomas and the Sisters of his mother's former convent.

Suddenly, Thomas' whole way of thinking was turned upside-down. Thomas was amazed that his mother had chosen a woman with breast cancer to tell him, in a way that could leave no doubt, that death is not the end and the spirit survives.

If you're like many people, you probably thought this story was going to be about healing associated with a woman who had battled cancer and celebrated five years of being cancer-free. But as it turned out, the story was about the healing of a young man's doubts about God and the afterlife.

As we continue our life journeys this week, it would be a good idea to reflect on our own lives. What kind of healing and care do we need in our life realms? What opportunities does God give us to practice healing and care in our lives?

And that is the good news I have for you on this Thirteenth Sunday in Ordinary Time.

Story source: Thomas Brown, "The Message," in Canfield & Hansen's *Chicken Soup for the Soul: Stories of Faith,* 2008, #97-99.

Chapter 37

14th Sunday in Ordinary Time - B
Mary McLeod Bethune

Scripture:

- Ezekiel 2: 2-5
- Psalm 123: 1-2a, 2bcd, 3-4
- 2 Corinthians 12: 7-10
- Mark 6: 1-6

Today, Catholic Christians celebrate the Fourteenth Sunday in Ordinary Time.

In St. Paul's second letter to the Corinthians (2 Corinthians 12: 7-10), we read how Paul had what he considered to be a "thorn in the flesh." Paul asked God three times to remove this "thorn," but God said, "My grace is sufficient for you, for power is made perfect in weakness" (2 Corinthians 12: 9). Once Paul realized that his "weakness" was actually a source of strength, he said, "I will rather boast most gladly of my weakness, in order that the power of Christ may dwell with me. Therefore, I am content with weaknesses, insults, hardships, persecutions, and constraints, for the sake of Christ; for when I am weak, then I am strong" (2 Corinthians 12: 9-10).

No one knows what Paul meant by "a thorn in the side." Many Bible scholars and others have tried to guess through the centuries what Paul meant by this. No one knows the real answer, but that is not important. What is important is what God had to say: "My grace is sufficient for you, for power is made perfect in weakness" (2 Corinthians 12: 9).

We should not be surprised at God's teaching, for we know that in Christianity, Jesus was frequently saying things that turned common understandings upside down. For example, he said that to be the leader, one must be the servant. He also said that the first shall be last, and the last shall be first.

In modern times, we have encountered many people who illustrate beautifully how one can have a quality that some consider a "weakness," and turn it into a great strength. Bill Wilson, for example, took his alcoholism and turned it into one of the greatest spiritual movements of the twentieth century – Alcoholics Anonymous. And from that movement came many other groups that use the 12-step spirituality. We also see how a Frenchman named Louis Braille, with his failing eyesight, created the Braille alphabet for the blind. Today, we look at a heroic American woman who used her sense of inequality to improve the lives of millions of African Americans. Her name was Mary McLeod Bethune.

Mary McLeod was born in a log cabin in Mayesville, South Carolina on July 10 1875. She was number 15 of 17 children. Though Mary was not born into slavery, many of her older brothers and sisters had been.

As a child, she worked with the rest of the family in the cotton fields of South Carolina. Her mother made a little money as a laundress, and

Mary McLeod went with her mother to deliver white people's laundry. One day, in a white family's home, she looked at a book. A white child of the family grabbed the book out of her hands, telling her that she couldn't read, so she should leave the book alone. That is when Mary noticed that the biggest difference between the black children and the white children was that the white children could read and write. Mary thought that this was unfair, and God planted a strong passion in her heart not only to learn to read and write, but to teach other black children to do so.

So, when she was 11 years old, Mary walked five miles to a one-room schoolhouse for black children. Because she was the only one in her family who went to school, each day she would come home and teach the other kids what she had learned in school that day. So, in effect, she became a "teacher" when she was just 11 years old.

When Mary grew up, she married Albertus Bethune in 1898 and lived in Georgia and Florida. Albertus left the family in 1907 and died in 1918.

In 1905, Mary opened – with just $1.50 - the Daytona, Florida Literary and Industrial School for Training Negro Girls. At first, the school had only six students: five girls and Mary's son Albert. For the next 25 years, however, the little school grew into a high school, and then into a junior college, and then into Bethune College. In 1931, the Methodist Church helped the college merge with a men's college called Cookman Institute. By 1941, the institute became a fully accredited four-year college, and today, the institution that Mary founded is known as Bethune-Cookman University in Daytona Beach, Florida. Mary served as President of the college from 1931 through 1942.

Though Mary McLeod Bethune devoted most of her life to education, she also helped African Americans in many other ways. As a close friend of President Franklin Delano Roosevelt and his wife Eleanor, Mary formed a group of black leaders that would come to be known as the "Black Cabinet," a group advising the president on matters of importance to African Americans.

Mary died on May 18, 1955 in Daytona Beach, Florida. She is celebrated in American history as an educator, author, and African American civil rights leader.

Like St. Paul, Mary Bethune took what she might have seen as a negative in her life, and used it to help millions of people.

As we continue our life journeys this week, it would be a good idea to reflect on our own lives. Do we have anything that we consider to be a "thorn" in our lives? How can we use that to grow, flourish, and help others?

And that is the good news I have for you on this Fourteenth Sunday in Ordinary Time.

Story sources:

• Dennis Denenberg & Lorraine Roscoe, "Mary McLeod Bethune," in *50 American Heroes Every Kid Should Know,* Minneapolis, Minnesota: Millbrook Press, 2006, pp. 20-21.
• "Mary McLeod Bethune," in *Wikipedia.*

Chapter 38

15th Sunday in Ordinary Time - B
The Nurse as Paraclete

Scripture:

- Amos 7: 12-15
- Psalm 85: 9ab & 10, 11-12, 13-14
- Ephesians 1: 3-14
- Mark 6: 7-13

Today, Catholic Christians celebrate the Fifteenth Sunday in Ordinary Time.

On this day, we read a short vocation story in the Book of Amos. In this account, a priest named Amaziah told Amos to become a prophet. Amaziah said, "Off with you, visionary, flee to the land of Judah! There earn your bread by prophesying…" (Amos 7:12). Amos replied, "I was no prophet, nor have I belonged to a company of prophets; I was a shepherd and a dresser of sycamores. The Lord took me from following the flock, and said to me, Go, prophesy to my people Israel" (Amos 7: 14-15).

This story is very important because it teaches us some interesting and important things about vocations and God's role in our individual vocations. In the case of Amos, God chose him to do work for which he had no education or background, but Amos believed that God was with him in his new vocation. In other words, God served as a Paraclete for Amos.

A paraclete is someone who advocates for us or stands beside us in times of trouble. Lawyers are often seen as paracletes when they stand beside their clients in a court of law. They speak on behalf of their clients. Sometimes, paracletes are seen as people who do things for us when we cannot do them for ourselves. Nurses, for example, often take on the role of a paraclete as we see in the following story by David Seamands.

There was once a man who had to have very serious open-heart surgery. On the day before the surgery, a nurse came into his room to do some pre-operative teaching. First, she took his hand in hers and said, "I want you to feel what my hand feels like."

Then, she said, "Tomorrow, when you are in surgery, you will be disconnected from your heart, and certain machines will be keeping you alive. When your heart is finally restored and the operation is all over, you will eventually wake up in a very special recovery room. You will be immobilized for as long as six hours. During that time, you will not be able to move, or speak, or even open your eyes. However, you will be conscious and you will hear everything that is going on around you. It is can be scary to be able to hear but not be able to communicate. So, during those six hours, I will be at your side, and I will hold your hand, exactly as I am doing now. I will stay with you until you are fully recovered.

Although you may feel absolutely helpless, when you feel my hand, you will know that you are okay and that I will not leave you."

After the man's surgery, the man experienced everything that the nurse had told him would happen. He woke up, but he could do nothing. But he was able to feel the nurse's hand in his hand for hours. And that made all the difference in the world. Instead of being terrified, he was comforted. He knew that as long as the nurse was present, all would be well.

This beautiful story ties in well with the story from Amos, for it can teach us many things. Here are just three.

First, God often calls us to do something with our lives for which we are unprepared. Imagine how poor Amos must have felt. After all, what does being a shepherd and a dresser of sycamore trees have to do with being a prophet? Probably the only thing we can answer is that God's ways are not our ways. What God can see in others, we often miss.

When we think we are unprepared for our vocations, we should take comfort in the fact that we are not alone. After all, I would imagine that just about every parent who ever lived did not know what he or she was doing when they started out as parents.

And in professions, people just coming out of school frequently feel they are actually "frauds." They may say, "Well, though I have a credential after my name, I don't really know what I'm doing." Like all new professionals, they are called to "fake it till they make it." That means they need to act like they know what they're doing until the day comes when they actually know what they're doing.

Second, we need to be prepared for God's call at any time in our lives. History is filled with people whom God called to do something special with their lives when they were advanced in age. Think, for example, of Grandma Moses, the great American folk artist, who didn't begin painting in earnest until she was 78 years old. Because many are living longer and longer lives today than in the past, we should expect God to ask us to different things at different times of our lives – even in our sunset years.

And third, we need to trust that God is with us as the Divine Paraclete. There is a beautiful saying that reflects this theology: "The will of God will not take you where the grace of God will not protect you." We must trust that if God wants us to do something in our lives, he will be like the nurse in the story, standing beside us to let us know we are not alone and that we are okay.

As we continue our life journeys this week, it would be a good idea to reflect on our own lives. How many times in our lives have we not known what we are doing in our vocations? How did God show us that he was with us in these times of doubt and uncertainty?

And that is the good news I have for you on this Fifteenth Sunday in Ordinary Time.

Story source: David Seamands, "Paraclete," in Alice Gray (Ed.), *Stories for the Heart: 110 Stories to Encourage Your Soul.* Gresham, Oregon: Vision House Publishing, Inc., 1996, p. 278.

Chapter 39

16th Sunday in Ordinary Time - B
St. Romuald

Scripture:

- Jeremiah 23: 1-6
- Psalm 23: 1-3a, 3b-4, 5, 6
- Ephesians 2: 13-18
- Mark 6: 30-34

Today, Catholic Christians celebrate the Sixteenth Sunday in Ordinary Time.

On this day, we read an interesting story from the Gospel of Mark. In this story, we find the disciples returning from doing missionary work in other places, eagerly telling their missionary stories to Jesus. Jesus knew they must be tired, so he said, "Come away by yourselves to a deserted place and rest a while" (Mark 6: 31).

Unfortunately for the Jesus and the disciples, people began coming toward them in such great numbers, that Jesus and his missionaries did not even have time to eat. Therefore, to get a little rest from their ministry, they got into a boat to head to a secluded place to find some time for contemplation.

But the people who had been trying to get to Jesus and his disciples saw them leave in the boat, and followed the shoreline until they arrived at the place where the boat was headed. We then read, "When he disembarked and saw the vast crowd, his heart was moved with pity for them, for they were like sheep without a shepherd; and he began to teach them many things" (Mark 6: 34).

Although this story contains a number of themes, today I focus on the necessity for contemplation in the spiritual life. One man who valued contemplation to a high degree was Romuald, who lived from around 951 to 1027.

Romuald was born in Ravenna, Italy. As a youth, Romuald lived the worldly life of a nobleman. At the age of twenty, however, something happened that changed his life forever. His father had a duel with another relative over some property, and Romuald's father killed the man. Romuald was so horrified by the event, that he went to a local basilica to do forty days of penance.

During his stay at the basilica, Romuald was called to become a monk in the monastery there. Unfortunately, Romuald was not sufficiently modest. He was overly zealous, and he believed the monks were not strict enough. His air of moral superiority made the other monks angry with him, so when he applied for permission to retire to Venice, they were thrilled to give him permission.

In Venice, he placed himself under the direction of a hermit named Marinus and lived an extremely severe lifestyle.

For several years, Romuald alternated between the life of a hermit and the comparatively more social life of a monk. For 30 years, he wandered all over Italy founding and reforming hermitages and monasteries.

One day, a friend of Romuald named Maldolus had a vision of white-robed monks ascending into heaven. After receiving the vision, Maldolus gave Romuald a gift of land that was to become known as Campus Maldoli or Camaldoli. There, Romuald built five cells for hermits. Years later, the campus became the well-known motherhouse of the Camaldolese Order of hermit-monks.

Romuald put a great emphasis on contemplative prayer. He said, "Sit in your cell as in paradise. Put the whole world behind you and forget it. Watch your thoughts like a good fisherman watching for fish. The path you must follow is in the Psalms – never leave it."

St. Romuald died on June 19, 1027, and his feast day is celebrated on June 19th.

The Camaldolese Order, which is part of the Benedictine family of monks, still exists. However, this has never been an Order of great numbers. In the United States, there are two groups of Camaldolese hermit-monks. The larger of the two groups is in Big Sur, California, and the smaller is in Bloomfield, Ohio.

From the Gospel reading and the life of St. Romuald, we can glean some important points. Here are just three.

First, most people are "shepherds" in a Biblical sense. Jesus is the Good Shepherd, head of the whole Christian Church. The pope is head of the earthly Catholic Church, bishops are heads of dioceses, pastors are shepherds of parishes, parents are shepherds of the domestic church or family, and big brothers and sisters are shepherds of young siblings. Even little children shepherd pets and their dolls. Thus, the concept of shepherding is very important for most of us in everyday life.

Second, today, contemplation is more important than ever. Unlike days past, many people in advanced societies like the United States are never away from work and communication sources. They are "socially connected" even when they are alone in their, and the idea of getting away for an extended vacation is a distant memory. This constant bombardment of stimuli can leave us emotionally drained, cranky, and even sick in mind, body, or spirit.

Contemplation, as I define it, means simply focusing on God's presence. This requires us to be quiet, to leave the thoughts and cares of the world behind, and just spend time with God.

And third, to have a balanced spiritual life, we need both active and passive elements. Just as we need a heart and brain to make the hands and legs work, we need a solid prayer life to allow us to be the missionaries that God has called all Christians to be.

As we continue our life journeys this week, it would be a good idea to reflect on how well we take time to simply sit and bask in the presence of God.

And that is the good news I have for you on this Sixteenth Sunday in Ordinary Time.

Story source: "St. Romuald," in *Butler's Lives of the Saints: June – New Full Edition,* Revised by Kathleen Jones, 1997, Collegeville, Minnesota, Burns & Oates, The Liturgical Press, pp. 133-134.

Chapter 40

17th Sunday in Ordinary Time - B
Drawn to the Warmth

Scripture:

- 2 Kings 4: 42-44
- Psalm 145: 10-11, 15-16, 17-18
- Ephesians 4: 1-6
- John 6: 1-15

Today, Catholic Christians celebrate the Seventeenth Sunday in Ordinary Time.

In today's second reading, in his letter to the Ephesians, St. Paul writes, "Brothers and sisters: I, a prisoner for the Lord, urge you to live in a manner worthy of the call you have received" (Ephesians 4: 1).

When Paul talks about "the call" we have received, he is referring to our vocations as Christians. We live this vocation not only by proclaiming Jesus as our Lord and Savior, but also by what Paul calls our manner of living,

As Christians, the ultimate guide for life is the triple love command of Jesus – to love God, our neighbor, and our selves.

Sometimes, we get the false idea that our Christian call requires us to do spectacular things. But as we know, most of life is routine, not spectacular.

Also, sometimes we get so caught up in the struggles of everyday life, that we simply forget how very special our Christian vocation is. Therefore, it is always a good idea to have a concrete example every once in a while of someone whose light shines brightly through everyday actions. That is what we see in the following story by Marion Smith called "Drawn to the Warmth."

This story takes place on a bitterly cold winter's day in Washington, D.C. A tourist from California, trying to get warmed up, ducked into Union Station and sat on one of the benches. As she waited for her fingers and toes to get warm, she enjoyed watching all the people coming and going from trains, buses, and restaurants in the station.

As the tourist watched, she noticed a very poor young man nearby. The man's body was gaunt, and he wore the tattered clothes of a homeless person. The tourist wondered how long it had been since the man had eaten.

As she wondered about this, the tourist could detect delicious smells of food coming from the restaurants, and she wondered if the poor young man was about to beg for some money. The homeless man, however, did not ask for anything.

As the tourist was debating whether or not she should go to the food court to buy the young man some food, or whether she should just mind her own business and not get involved, a well-dressed young couple approached the homeless man and said, "Excuse me, sir. My wife and I just finished eating in a local restaurant, and we weren't as hungry as we thought. We hate to waste good food. Would you help us out and put this to use?" The couple gave the homeless man a large Styrofoam container.

"God bless you both. Merry Christmas!" the homeless young man said.

The young homeless man was beside himself with joy. He examined his new meal with the care he would examine a jewelry case of fine diamonds. He rearranged the soup crackers, inspected the club sandwich, and stirred the salad dressing. He was obviously trying to make the meal last a long time, for it was truly a rare treat.

At last, the young homeless man took off the lid of his soup, cupped his hands around the steaming warm bowl, and inhaled the delicious aroma. But just as he was lifting the soup to his mouth, he stopped and looked up. There, we saw an elderly man in lightweight pants, a threadbare jacket and open shoes. His hands were raw, and looked like he was freezing.

Suddenly, the young homeless man set his meal aside, jumped up, and guided the elderly man to an adjacent seat. He took the elderly man's icy hands in his and rubbed them briskly. He took off his own worn jacket and put it over the old man's shoulders.

The young man then said, "Pop, my name's Jack, and a couple of God's angels brought me this meal. I just finished eating and hate to waste good food. Can you help me out?"

Jack put the still-warm bowl of soup in the old man's hands without waiting for an answer.

The old man said, "Sure, son, but only if you go halfway with me on that sandwich. It's too much for a man my age."

The tourist, who witnessed all of this, was amazed. She was also thoroughly ashamed of herself. She called herself a "Christian," but she was the only one in the scenario who had not shown the love that a Christian should show. Therefore, she promptly got up, walked to the food court, and came out to the two homeless men to give them some large containers of coffee and a big assortment of pastries. She left Union Station warmed up not only in body, but also in spirit.

This beautiful story shows Christianity in action — from the young couple's giving their leftover food to the young homeless man, to the young homeless man offering the food to the older man, and the older man insisting the younger man share half.

Though we may not find ourselves in the midst of homeless persons who are hungry on a winter night, we have an incredible number of opportunities to serve others. So, as we continue our life journeys this week, it would be a good idea to reflect on those around us who may need a little help on their journeys. How can we help?

And that is the good news I have for you on this Seventeenth Sunday in Ordinary Time.

Story source: Smith, Marion. "Drawn to the Warmth" in Canfield, Hansen, and Newmark (Eds.), *Chicken Soup for the Soul: Stories of Faith,* Cos Cob, Connecticut, Chicken Soup for the Soul Publishing, 2008, pp. 226-227.

Chapter 41

18th Sunday in Ordinary Time - B
Nobody's Perfect

Scripture:

- Exodus 16: 2-4, 12-15
- Psalm 78: 3 & 4bc, 23-24, 25 & 54
- Ephesians 4: 17, 20-24
- John 6: 24-35

Today, Catholic Christians celebrate the Eighteenth Sunday in Ordinary Time.

On this day, St. Paul writes to the church in Ephesus. He tells the people that they should reform their lives. In part, he says, "...you should put away the old self of your former way of life, corrupted through deceitful desires, and be renewed in the spirit of your minds, and put on the new self, created in God's way in righteousness and holiness of truth" (Ephesians 4: 22-24).

This writing by St. Paul is very important, because it calls us to consider some basic tenets of our faith. Before exploring them, however, let's look at the following letter written by a man who was applying to be the preacher of the local Christian church.

> *Dear Personnel Committee,*
>
> *I heard that you have a position open for a preacher. I would very much like to be considered for the job. It is true, that my preaching usually stirs up a lot of controversy. In fact, one of my sermons actually caused a riot. Also, I have a hard time keeping a job and am never in one place for more than 3 years.*
>
> *My health isn't great. In fact, I have something I call a "thorn in my side." And, to be honest, I'm not all that handsome. However, I don't think this fact has made my preaching any less effective.*
>
> *I am a lifelong bachelor and have no children. In fact, I preach that being single is a much holier state than being married. Nevertheless, I am surprisingly good at conducting family life seminars.*
>
> *If you do a background check on me – and I'm sure you will – you probably will discover that I changed my name after I gave up being a terrorist. Even today, I end up in jail a lot. But please, don't overreact. I'm a changed person in spite of everything. In fact, many people tell me I'm a wonderful theologian even though I have never been to a seminary.*
>
> *I hope you aren't looking for a good administrator, because I'm not good at that. In fact, I forget things all the time. I am, however, a hard worker, and that should count for something.*

In my life, I have found out that even when I don't do too well in my work, everything seems to work out in the end. I guess that is because God is watching over me.

Well, that's about it. Please let me know if you are interested in hiring me to be your preacher. I can start next week.
Sincerely,
Paul of Tarsus, formerly known as Saul

So, would you hire this man? I hope so, because it is the apostle Paul, the man whose writing we read every Sunday when we come to church. In fact, Catholic Christians, like most Christians, base most of their theology on the writings of this man!

Today, for example, St. Paul is telling the people to reform their lives. This idea has led our church to form many guidelines for doing exactly this. Here are just three.

First, there is no such thing as a "hopeless case" in the spiritual life. In other words, all of us are capable of being better and better persons. All of us are called to grow and flourish like the little mustard seed that became a huge bush. Now some people say that people can't change. They even have a saying, "A leopard can't change its spots." Well, maybe leopards can't change their spots, but humans can change. We can become better persons by adding virtues to our lives and by removing vices. We change by developing our talents through studying and through life experiences. For the Christian, striving for perfection is an ongoing process.

Second, we should never judge others, for we cannot know their whole story. We don't know where they have been, and we don't know where they are going. Before he became Paul, Saul was a terrorist. He loved to persecute the Christian Church. If someone looked at him during his terrorist days and labeled him as "unchangeable," they would have been sadly mistaken.

And third, often the challenges we have faced, and the battles we have won, make us the ideal persons to help others in like situations. Recovering alcoholics and other addicts are often the very best addiction counselors, for they have not only read about the conditions they are treating, they have experienced them. They have first-hand knowledge, and that is the very best teacher one can have.

As we continue our life journeys this week, it would be a good idea to reflect on how we are growing and flourishing. What obstacles have we overcome in our lives, and how have those victories made us better ministers?

And that is the good news I have for you on this Eighteenth Sunday in Ordinary Time.

Story source: Anonymous. "Well, Nobody's Perfect." In Wayne Rice, *Still More Hot Illustrations for Youth Talks,* Grand Rapids, Michigan, Youth Specialties/Zondervan, 1999, pp. 40-41.

Chapter 42

19th Sunday in Ordinary Time - B
Children for Peace

Scripture:

- 1 Kings 19: 4-8
- Psalm 34: 2-3, 4-5, 6-7, 8-9
- Ephesians 4: 30 – 5: 2
- John 6: 41-51

Today, Catholic Christians celebrate the Nineteenth Sunday in Ordinary Time.

On this day, we read about the need for unity among the followers of Christ. In his letter to the Ephesians, St. Paul says, "All bitterness, fury, anger, shouting, and reviling must be removed from you, along with all malice. And be kind to one another, compassionate, forgiving one another as God has forgiven you in Christ" (Ephesians 4: 31-32).

Though the words of St. Paul seem clear, they are not easy to put into practice. For over 2,000 years, the Church has struggled to achieve unity and to have its members be kind and compassionate toward one another. The good news, however, is that God always sends us people filled with the Holy Spirit, people whose light shines so brightly, that they light the dark pathways of the world for others to follow.

In the following story reported by Garth Sundem, we hear the true story of a heroic teenager from Colombia. Her name was Farliz Calle.

Farliz was a personable teenager with sparkling eyes and a winning smile. Everybody liked her. In fact, she was the president of the student council in her school. Her father picked bananas at a nearby plantation, and her mother cooked for plantation workers. Farliz had two sisters, a brother, and many friends. She dreamed of one day becoming a criminal psychologist.

Like most teenagers, Farliz had worries. Her worries, however, were very serious. She worried that one day her father might go to work and be shot. She worried that the lives of the adults and children in her town of Apartadó were in danger because of the war between the Colombian government and gangs that had been going on for 50 years. During those years, Farliz knew that over 300,000 people had been killed because of the fighting. She also knew that in the capital city of Bogotá, car bombings and kidnappings were common.

Despite the violence all around her, Farliz dreamed of the day there would be peace, when people could sleep at night without hearing gunfire. She dreamed of the day when children could play in the streets without worry about being kidnapped by gangs. Though she didn't know what she could possibly do as a teenager, she knew that there must be something.

Then one day, a woman from the United Nations came to town. Farliz organized a greeting and exhibition of poems, stories, sculptures, letters, and paintings for the United Nations representative, all done by youth. The representative, Graca Machel, was deeply moved. When she went back to the United Nations, she reported what she had discovered. From this, the Children's Peace Movement was born.

Farliz soon found others who wanted to help. Among them was Juan Elías Uribe, who wanted peace on behalf of his physician father who had been killed when he spoke out against the violence. Mayerly Sánchez also joined the movement after a Colombian gang murdered her best friend. Wolfido Zambrano joined because he was tired of seeing dead bodies in the streets of Apartadó. Dilio Lorenzo joined and said, "Enough is enough, and we won't accept this anymore. We demand change." None of the people helping Farliz were more than sixteen years old.

Soon, Farliz and her followers realized they had outgrown the student government. They also learned that according to the Colombian constitution, people could petition to vote for anything. So, the Children's Peace Movement sought to get 500,000 youth to join the movement and vote for the "right to survival, peace, family, and freedom from abuse." On October 25, 1996, after only six months of seeking members, the group reported that it had gotten 2.7 million youth to join them!

Of course not everybody in Colombia was happy with this group. Some of the most dangerous people in the country were against the youth and their peace movement.

Daily, the youth leaders received death threats. Therefore, the Children's Peace Movement's leaders never say the name of a gang; that way, they can live to see another day.

One year after the historic children's vote, ten million of the adults of Colombia voted for peace. Though war continues, violence is decreasing in this country. Farliz was nominated for the Nobel Peace Prize in 1999. She sums up the goals of the Children's Peace Movement this way: "We request to all the adults of all the countries in the world: Peace in the world. Peace in our countries. Peace in our homes. Peace in our hearts."

Although you and I do not face the same amount of daily violence as Farliz and her friends did, we also have challenges. We too must follow the ideals of Christ, becoming people of love, kindness, compassion, mercy, forgiveness, gentleness, humility, and charity. We too must strive to eliminate hatred from our hearts and to see Christ in every human being.

One thing we can always count on is never running out of opportunities to practice the Christian virtues in our everyday lives.

As we continue our lives this week, it would be a good idea to reflect on how we are trying to build unity in our parish community and larger community at large.

And that is the good news I have for you on this Nineteenth Sunday in Ordinary Time.

Story source: Garth Sundem, "When Small Voices Unite," *Real Kids, Real Stories, Real Change: Courageous Actions Around the World,* Minneapolis, Minnesota, Free Spirit Publishing, Inc., 2010, pp. 39-43.

Chapter 43

20th Sunday in Ordinary Time - B
The Farmer's 3 Wishes

Scripture:

- Proverbs 9: 1-6
- Psalm 34: 2-3, 4-5, 6-7
- Ephesians 5: 15-20
- John 6: 51-58

Today, Catholic Christians celebrate the Twentieth Sunday in Ordinary Time.

On this day, we read a selection from St. Paul's letter to the Church in Ephesus. In the letter, he gives the Christians advice on how to live as good followers of Christ. In today's passage, he ends his discourse by telling the people that they should be "…giving thanks always and for everything in the name of our Lord Jesus Christ to God the Father" (Ephesians 5: 20).

Giving thanks to God is a theme sprinkled throughout the Bible in both Old and New Testaments, and it is something seen in every religion. Before discussing the concept in greater detail, however, let us look at an ancient Jewish parable called "The Farmer's Three Wishes."

One night, an angel of the Lord awakened a poor farmer. The angel said, "God has found favor with you, so he would like to reward you as he did for your ancestor Abraham. As a reward, God will grant you three wishes. There is only one condition: your neighbor will get a double portion of everything that is given to you."

The farmer was, of course, amazed by this news, so he woke up his wife and told her all about it. The farmer's wife insisted that they test this promise to see if it was actually real and not just a dream. So, they prayed that God would give them a herd of 1,000 cattle so that they would no longer be poor.

No sooner had they asked this, than they heard the sound of animal noises outside. They were amazed to see cattle all around the house and in their fields. For the next two days, the farmer was so thrilled that he spent all his time praising God for his generosity.

On the third day, while atop a hill trying to decide where he could build a new barn, the farmer looked across at his neighbor's field. There, he saw 2,000 cattle that God had given his neighbor. Now, instead of a heart filled with joy and gratitude, his heart filled with envy toward his neighbor. He could not eat, and he went to bed in a rage. Instead of focusing on his 1,000 cattle, he could only think of his neighbor's 2,000 cattle.

The next day, however, he remembered that he could have two wishes more. Therefore, he examined his heart very carefully. He remembered that he had always wanted descendants to carry on the family name. Therefore, he prayed for a child. In just a couple of days, his wife told him that she was pregnant. Suddenly his heart was once again filled with joy and thanksgiving. On the night his first child was born, his joy was complete. The next day, he went to the synagogue to give thanks to God for the child. He had just finished his prayer of thanksgiving, however, when his neighbor came into the synagogue and said, "Thanks be to God! Last night my wife gave birth to twin sons!"

The farmer's joy suddenly left him, and he became filled with rage and envy. This time, his dark emotions did not leave him. They only grew worse. Therefore, late in the evening, he made his third request to God: "Lord, please gouge out my right eye." He knew, of course, that his neighbor would then become blind, for the angel had promised the neighbor would receive double of whatever the farmer asked for.

The angel, with tears in his eyes, asked the farmer why he had asked for such a terrible thing. The farmer replied, "I can't stand to see my neighbor prosper! I'll gladly sacrifice half of my vision for the satisfaction of knowing that he'll become blind and never be able to look on what he has."

The angel said, "I'm sorry, but God will not grant your third wish. It is not because God lacks integrity, but because he is full of mercy. However, know this, you foolish man, you have brought sadness not only to yourself, but to the very heart of God."

This story ties in well with today's reading from St. Paul to the Ephesians, for it reminds us of certain points to keep in mind when considering being thankful.

First, we are called to give thanks to God for all of our blessings. Giving thanks is a behavior, an action that comes from an act of the will, not from an emotional state. Therefore, even when we don't particularly feel thankful for what we have is no excuse for not thanking God for what we have.

Second, having hearts of gratitude means we try to be satisfied with what we have. There will always be people who have more than we have: looks, brains, ambition, jobs, education, luck, money, houses, and other things. That does not mean we should be ungrateful for what we have. We should instead consider what we do have and try to feel satisfied.

And third, we should rejoice in the good fortune of others. The second part of Jesus' triple-love commandment is that we are to love others. To "love" others means we wish the best for them. Having God shower them with blessings should be an answer to our prayer for them, not a source of envy.

As we continue our life journeys this week, it would be a good idea to reflect on all of our blessings. Do we thank God every day for what we have? Are we satisfied with our blessings? Do we harbor envy or jealousy in our hearts toward others?

And that is the good news I have for you on this Twentieth Sunday in Ordinary Time.

Story source: John Claypool, "The Farmer's Three Wishes," In Wayne Rice, *Still More Hot Illustrations for Youth Talks, Grand* Rapids, Michigan: Youth Specialties/Zondervan, 1999, pp. 98-100.

Chapter 44

21st Sunday in Ordinary Time - B
Honoring Her Husband

Scripture:

- Joshua 24: 1-2a, 15-17, 18b
- Psalm 34: 2-3, 16-17, 18-19, 20-21
- Ephesians 5: 21-32
- John 6: 60-69

Today, Catholic Christians celebrate the Twenty-First Sunday in Ordinary Time.

On this day, we read a very famous, and often controversial, section from St. Paul's letter to the Ephesians. In this section, Paul is trying to give the Ephesian Christians points on how to have a holy marriage.

The part that is problematic to many people today is when he says, "Wives should be subordinate to their husbands as to the Lord. For the husband is head of his wife just as Christ is head to the church, he himself is the savior of the body. As the church is subordinate to Christ, so wives should be subordinate to their husbands in everything" (Ephesians 5: 22-24).

Before examining this particular passage in greater detail, let's look at a very old story called "Honoring Her Husband." The story strives to illustrate the idea of "honor within marriage."

One evening, a drunken husband – whom I'll call Patrick - was spending time with his equally drunk friends in a tavern. Patrick was bragging to the other men that if he took them to home at midnight and asked his Christian wife to get up and cook a dinner for them, she would do so without a complaint. The other men considered this to be a vain boast, so they dared Patrick to try it.

Patrick accepted the challenge and took the drunken crowd home. When they got to Patrick's house, he woke up his wife, Bridget, and made the unreasonable demand that she get up and prepare a big dinner for him and his guests.

Bridget got up, got dressed, came down to the kitchen, and prepared a delicious dinner. She served it very cheerfully as though she had been expecting the crowd all along.

After the dinner, one of the men asked Bridget how she could be so kind when her husband had been so unreasonable and when she obviously did not approve of his drunken conduct. Bridget replied, "Well, sir, when my husband and I got married, we were both sinners. It pleased God to call me out of that dangerous condition. My husband, though, continues to live a sinful life. I tremble for his future state. Were he to die as he is, he would be miserable forever. I think it is my duty to make his present existence as comfortable as possible."

Not long after Bridget's speech, Patrick turned his life to God as his wife had done.

We now go back to Paul's problematic passage of wives being subordinate to their husbands. When many Christians encounter such Bible passages that go against our modern-day values such as gender equality, they often simply ignore such passages and try to change the subject.

A better alternative is, I believe, to face it squarely and to examine in it terms of our Catholic faith. Here are just three points to keep in mind when reading this passage.

First, we should always be careful to not take passages from the Bible out of context. For example, the Bible says in Psalm 14, verse 1, "There is no God." Well, when we look at Psalm 14: 1 in greater detail, we read, "Fools say in their hearts, 'There is no God.' Their deeds are loathsome and corrupt; not one does what is right."

When we look at Paul's letter to the Ephesians, we realize that St. Paul also said, "Husbands, love your wives, even as Christ loved the church and handed himself over for her to sanctify her" (Ephesians 5: 25).

Second, we need to remember that Catholic Christians are not fundamentalists or biblical literalists. In fact, the Catholic worldview sees God, the world, and human beings as "intrinsically good," while fundamentalists often focus on the fallen nature of the human and the world.

Catholic Christians consider the cultural, temporal, and historical contexts in which the various books of the Bible were written. If we ignore those things, we cannot fully understand the basic message of many of the main teachings of the Bible. It would be incredible folly to judge the books of the Bible, written many centuries ago, using twenty-first century American thinking.

And third, even if you are so stuck on, and offended by, the idea of "wives be subordinate to your husbands," you'll be delighted to know that sociologists have discovered that it is the wife, not the husband, who is the head of the family in modern American families. Being "the head" means getting what one wants. Americans even have sayings that reflect this reality, sayings such as "Happy wife - happy life," and "If mama ain't happy, ain't nobody happy!" In everyday American life, we often hear men say, when asked if they can do a particular thing or go to a particular function, "I'll have to ask the boss." "The boss," in this case, is the wife.

I have never heard wives say, "I'll have to ask the boss" referring to their husband. The sociological research is quite solid, but it is beyond this homily.

As we continue our life journeys this week, it would be a good idea to reflect on our own lives. Is mutual respect present in our homes?

And that is the good news I have for you on this Twenty-First Sunday in Ordinary Time.

Story source: Anonymous, "Honoring Her Husband," in *Ministry 127*, World Wide Web, August 19, 2015.

Chapter 45

22nd Sunday in Ordinary Time - B
A Boy Named Selim

Scripture:

- Deuteronomy 4: 1-2, 6-8
- Psalm 15: 2-3a, 3bc-4ab, 5
- James 1: 17-18, 21b-22, 27
- Mark 7: 1-8, 14-15, 21-23

Today, Catholic Christians celebrate the Twenty-Second Sunday in Ordinary Time.

On this day, we read a nice variety of Scripture passages about God's laws and how we are to approach them. Certainly one of the main themes we see today, and which we'll come across in the next few Sundays, is that we are supposed to put our faith into action. It is not sufficient to be able to simply rattle off rules.

In the following ancient Iranian legend, we hear of a boy who put his faith into action to the astonishment of all.

There was once a boy named Selim who was a camel driver. One day, as Selim was traveling through the desert, a gang of robbers surrounded him and his caravan. The robbers called out, "Give us your money and jewels!"

Gradually, the thieves made their way down the line of camels to Selim, taking the treasures of Selim's fellow travelers. When the robbers got to Selim, they searched his pockets but did not find anything of value. The chief of the robbers asked Selim, "Don't you have any money or jewels, boy?"

Selim answered, "I have three gold coins that my mother sewed into the corner of my coat."

The chief robber was astonished at the answer Selim gave him and said, "But why did you tell me that? I never would have found them there!"

Selim answered, "I told you this because my mother taught me to do three things in life. First, she told me to be kind to everyone. Second, she taught me to pray to God every day. And third, she told me to always tell the truth."

The robbers were amazed, for they had never met anyone who would tell the truth even if meant losing their money. The gang leader thought for a minute in silence. Then, he said to Selim, "Instead of taking your money, I am going to give you three gold coins. If my mother had taught me what yours taught you, I would not be a robber today. Instead, I would be supporting myself doing honest work."

The gang of robbers left Selim and his caravan in safety. And Selim left not only richer in things of this world, but also with a renewed sense of how precious the values his mother taught him actually were.

In today's Scripture readings, we hear many interesting and solid ideas we can use in our daily lives. If we keep these in mind and put them into practice, we will be closer to achieving a sense of serenity. And the older we get, the more we realize that serenity is more priceless than all the treasures on earth. Here are three things we can glean from today's readings.

First, in the Book of James, we learn that we need to put our faith into action. Specifically, James says, "Be doers of the word and not just hearers only, deluding yourselves" (James 1: 22). To make his point even clearer, James continues, "Religion that is pure and undefiled before God and the Father is this: to care for orphans and widows in their afflictions and to keep oneself unstained by the world" (James 1: 27).

Many take great delight in studying the Scriptures as an academic exercise. They love to show off their knowledge by reciting all of the books of the Bible in order, memorizing Bible verses, and informing others in which Book of the Bible various themes are located. I'm never impressed with this, for I know that all of that information is on my computer, information that I can look up any time I want.

I am impressed, on the other hand, when people put their faith in action in daily life. For example, I don't care whether people know where Jesus' teaching about forgiving one's enemies is located. I am impressed, on the other hand, by watching people forgive those who have harmed them. When they do this, they are imitating Jesus Christ.

Second, we should see God's laws as something good and freeing, something that will allow us to walk through the world as very special people – people of the Lord. In today's selection from the Book of Deuteronomy, God gives the people "statutes and decrees" so that they can take possession of the Promised Land. God says that if the Hebrew people observe these commands, they will be blessed. God says, "Observe them carefully, for thus will you give evidence of your wisdom and intelligence to the nations, who will hear of all these statutes and say, 'This great nation is truly a wise and intelligent people'" (Deuteronomy 4: 6).

And third, we learn that we are to be careful to not cling to human traditions that take us away from God's laws. In today's selection from St. Mark, for example, Jesus says, "You disregard God's commandment but cling to human tradition" (Mark 7: 8). This advice is just as important today as it was in the time of Jesus. Today, we have taken cultural customs and made them into idols. For example, discriminating against people on the basis of race, gender, sexual orientation, age, financial status, etc. show contempt for the idea of loving of neighbor. Such cultural customs violate the Golden Rule that Jesus taught: "Do to others whatever you would have them to do to you. This is the law and the prophets" (Matthew 7: 12).

As we continue our life journeys this week, it would be a good idea to reflect on how we see God's law of love. How do we love God, neighbor, and self in daily life?

And that is the good news I have for you on this Twenty-Third Sunday in Ordinary Time.

Story source: Anonymous "Selim," in Thomas W. Goodhue, *Sharing the Good News with Children: Stories for the Common Lectionary,* Cincinnati, Ohio, St. Anthony Messenger Press, 1992, p. 185.

Chapter 46

23rd Sunday in Ordinary Time - B
The Boot Cleaner

Scripture:

- Isaiah 35: 4-7a
- Psalm 146: 6c-7, 8-9a, 9bc-10
- James 2: 1-5
- Mark 7: 31-37

Today, Catholic Christians celebrate the Twenty-Third Sunday in Ordinary Time.

On this day, we hear a powerful message from the Letter of James about treating all people with equal dignity and respect. James says:

> ...show no partiality as you adhere to the faith in our glorious Lord Jesus Christ. For if a man with gold rings and fine clothes comes into your assembly, and a poor person in shabby clothes also comes in, and you pay attention to the one wearing the fine clothes and say, "Sit here, please," while you say to the poor one, "Stand there," or "Sit at my feet," have you not made distinctions among yourselves and become judges with evil designs? (James 2: 1-4)

This passage from St. James is vitally important to persons of all ages, because the temptation to place ourselves ahead of others is almost universal and can be seen throughout history.

In today's world, we often talk about "climbers," people who are driven to "climb the ladder" of success. Pope Francis condemns this quality in clergy, calling it "careerism." We'll discuss some ideas the pope has about this later. For now, however, let's look at the story of a young man who definitely had "careerist" dreams until, one day, he realized the folly of his thinking.

There was once a young man named Samuel Logan Brengle who lived from 1860 to 1936. When he was a college student, he found that he was quite brilliant in law and also had a remarkable gift of speaking.

One day, young Samuel felt God calling him to be a preacher. So, after receiving his Bachelor of Arts degree, he became a preacher in the Methodist Church. Because he was so effective as a preacher, his superiors recommended that he become a pastor of a large city church. They even said that one day he might even become a bishop.

Because of Samuel's success, he entered Boston Theological Seminary to pursue a Bachelor of Divinity degree before taking on more prestigious responsibilities. But around the time Samuel was living in Boston, a branch of the new Protestant missionary denomination called the Salvation Army was established in the city. Samuel was very attracted to this new group and went to England to meet the head of the organization.

Unfortunately for Samuel, he was full of pride that arose from all of the successes and praise that had been heaped on him.

His first assignment as a Salvation Army cadet was to sit in a small room and clean and shine boots of his 18 fellow cadets. As he faced the dirty boots, he thought of the potentially brilliant future he had given up in the Methodist Church. He wondered if he had made a serious mistake, wasting his time and talent, cleaning boots.

Then, he imagined Jesus kneeling on the floor, washing the dirty feet of his disciples. Samuel said, "I could see my Lord – who had come from the bosom of the everlasting father and the glories of heaven and the adoration of its hosts – bending over the feet of uncouth, unlearned fishermen, washing them, humbling Himself, taking the form of a servant. I immediately fell on my knees and prayed: 'Lord, you washed their feet; I will polish their boots.'"

Samuel did indeed learn the value of the servant-leadership model in ministry, and he went on to be a very famous author, teacher, and preacher in the Salvation Army.

Though we all know how important it is to treat all people with equal dignity and respect, this is often very difficult to do. Sometimes, pride and self-importance prevent us from treating others as "equals." Although this is a problem that all people must watch out for, those with exalted positions of authority and honor are particularly in danger. That is what Pope Francis has repeatedly warned Catholic bishops and cardinals about in many of his speeches.

Here are three points Pope Francis makes to bishops and cardinals to help them remember to strive for the humility of the servant-leadership model that Jesus taught.

First, the pope told the bishops to "tend the flock that is in your charge." To do that, the bishops must serve the flock, not themselves. Like Jesus, the Good Shepherd, bishops must offer their lives to their sheep. To do this, however, they must have accepting and loving hearts. This means not picking and choosing which people they will love and which they will reject.

Second, Pope Francis said that bishops must "walk with the flock." In other words, bishops must walk with the faithful and the priests, sharing in their dreams and joys and hopes and sufferings and difficulties. They must not be so far removed from the flock that they can't appreciate the everyday life experiences of those they are supposed to be serving.

And third, Pope Francis warns bishops not to fall into the "snare of careerism." He warns against bishops becoming ambitious, dreaming of having churches that are more beautiful or richer or more important. He specifically decries "airport bishops," bishops who are continually leaving their flock to fly around the world "being important," continually seeking recognition that would lead to promotions.

As we continue our life journeys this week, it would be good to examine our own hearts. Do we treat everyone with equal dignity and respect? How are we failing in this regard, and how can we improve?

And that is the good news I have for you on this Twenty-Third Sunday in Ordinary Time.

Story sources:

• Samuel Logan Brengle, *Sermon Central*, WWW, October 2006.
• "Pope Francis: 'Avoid the Scandal of Being Airport Bishops,'" ZENIT.org, September 19, 2013.

Chapter 47

24th Sunday in Ordinary Time - B
The Pastry Solution

Scripture:

- Isaiah 50: 5-9a
- Psalm 116: 1-2, 3-4, 5-6, 8-9
- James 2: 14-18
- Mark 8: 27-35

Today, Catholic Christians celebrate the Twenty-Fourth Sunday in Ordinary Time.

On this day, we hear from St. James, one of the most practical of all writers of the Bible. In today's selection, he reminds us that we need to put our faith into action to be effective. Specifically, James says:

> "What good is it, my brothers and sisters, if someone says he has faith but does not have works? Can that faith save him? If a brother or sister has nothing to wear and has no food for the day, and one of you says to them, 'Go in peace, keep warm, and eat well,' but you do not give them the necessities of the body, what good is it? So also faith of itself, if it does not have works, is dead" (James 2: 14-17).

In the following story by Steve Case, we see how one man indeed put his faith into action. Though it was not what others expected him to do, he not only demonstrated putting his faith into action, but he showed them how Christians are to treat those who are much poorer than themselves.

There was once a parish that we'll call St. Michael. It has always been a very wealthy parish. Even though it only had 300 members, the annual offertory was over one million dollars. The people had plenty of money, and they certainly could afford it.

Over the years, though, the neighborhood surrounding the beautiful old church and parish grounds had begun to change. Poor people from around the world flocked to the area, changing the complexion of the community. Soon, steel bars began replacing welcome signs in store windows. More and more homeless people could be seen wandering the area. Many of the St. Michael parishioners were very uncomfortable with the changes. Now, they began to avoid coming to the St. Michael neighborhood except to attend Mass on Sundays.

In the warm months, the parishioners loved to gather after Mass in the flower gardens outside the church, among its gazebos, fountains, and vine-covered arches. One Sunday, shortly after a young associate pastor had joined the church staff, the church members were gathered after the morning Mass for coffee and pastries.

As the elegantly dressed worshipers sipped coffee and visited with each other, a homeless man shuffled in off the street. He entered through the garden gate, trying to avoid eye contact with anyone. But everyone was looking at him. Quietly, he walked over to the table where expensive pastries were displayed on silver trays. He picked up one of the pastries and bit into it, keeping his eyes closed.

He then reached for a second pastry and put it into his coat pocket. Moving slowly and trying to not be noticed, he placed another into the same pocket.

The parishioners began talking among themselves. Finally, one woman walked over to the young priest and said, "Father, do something!"

Though the young priest was still not completely comfortable in his new position, he handed his coffee cup to the woman, walked over to the table, and greeted the homeless man. The priest then found two empty pastry boxes under the table. Picking up one of the silver trays filled with pastries, he emptied them into one of the boxes. Then he did the same with a second tray of pastries. He closed the lids on the boxes and held them out to the homeless man saying, "We're here every Sunday."

The man smiled at the young priest, cradled the boxes in his arms, and shuffled quietly out of the garden and down the street.

The young priest then returned to the woman, smiled as she gave back his coffee cup, and said, "That is what you meant when you said, 'Father, do something,' wasn't it?"

This beautiful story ties in well with today's message from St. James, for it reminds of many elements of Catholic social teaching. Here are just three such aspects.

First, we must put our faith into action. We have to "walk the walk," not just "talk the talk." Talk is cheap. If we don't live our faith, our "profession of faith" is pretty meaningless.

Second, the Catholic Church teaches that we are always to give a "preferential option for the poor." That means that the *needs* of the poor should always come before the *desires* of the rich. And because "catholic" means "universal," Catholic Christians are called to serve the needs of all people throughout the world; human-made national boundaries should make no difference in practicing our charity.

And third, we need to be careful about forming "cliques" in our parishes. While it is always comfortable to form friendships and enjoy being around certain people, we need to be careful that we don't exclude others just because they are not in our immediate circle of friends. We need to be ready to extend a smile and welcome to others of our community.

As we continue our life journeys this week, it would be a good idea to reflect on how we welcome others into our community. Are we always ready to extend a warm welcome to others? Are we always ready to put the needs of the poor ahead of our own desires?

And that is the good news I have for you on this Twenty-Fourth Sunday in Ordinary Time.

Story source: Steve Case, "Do Something," in Wayne Rice, *Hot Illustrations for Youth Talks,* Grand Rapids, Michigan: Youth Specialties/Zondervan, 2001, pp. 45-46.

Chapter 48

25th Sunday in Ordinary Time - B
The Miser

Scripture:

- Wisdom 2: 12, 17-20
- Psalm 54: 3-4, 5, 6 & 8
- James 3: 16 – 4: 3
- Mark 9: 30-37

Today, Catholic Christians celebrate the Twenty-Fifth Sunday in Ordinary Time.

On this day, Jesus teaches his disciples a very important lesson that would, through the ages, be the foundation of what today we call the "servant leadership model." We read in the Gospel of Mark: "They came to Capernaum and, once inside the house, he began to ask them, 'What were you arguing about on the way?' But they remained silent. They had been discussing among themselves on the way who was the greatest. Then he sat down, called the Twelve, and said to them, 'If anyone wishes to be first, he shall be the last of all and servant of all'" (Mark 9: 33-35).

The virtue Jesus was emphasizing was, of course, humility. Other models of leadership that were common in Jesus' day, as in our own, did not associate humility with leadership. Therefore, this was big news.

Fortunately, though, we have many examples of people doing good things while remaining humble. That is what we see in the following Jewish fable called, "The Miser."

There was once a rich Jewish man who never helped the poor of his town or contributed to any charitable causes. People in the small village didn't even call him by his name; they simply called him "The Miser."

One day, a beggar came to the door of The Miser and asked if he could have some money to buy food. The Miser asked the man where he was from, and the beggar replied that he was from the village. "Nonsense," replied The Miser. "You couldn't come from the village, for everyone in the village knows that I do not support beggars!" With that, he slammed the door on the poor beggar.

Now in the same village, there was a poor shoemaker. He was not only a very cheerful and friendly man, but also a very generous man. Any time that he heard of someone in the village who was in need, or that a charitable cause needed funds, he helped immediately. No one was ever turned away empty-handed from his door.

One day, The Miser died. The village elders decided to bury him at the edge of the cemetery. No one mourned his passing, and no one followed the funeral procession to the cemetery.

As the days passed, the village rabbi heard some disturbing news about the shoemaker. "He is no longer giving alms to beggars" complained one man. "He has refused every charity that has approached him," said another.

The rabbi asked, "Has anyone asked the shoemaker why he is no longer helping those in need?"

The people replied, "Yes. He says he no longer has any money."

So, the rabbi paid a visit to the shoemaker and asked, "Why have you suddenly stopped giving money to worthy causes?"

Slowly, the shoemaker began to speak. "Many years ago, the man you called The Miser came to me with a huge sum of money. He asked me to distribute the money to beggars and charities. He made me promise that I would not reveal the source of the money until after he died. Once a month, he would visit me secretly and give me additional money to distribute. I became known as a great benefactor even though I never spent a penny of my own money. I'm surprised that no one questioned me earlier. How could anyone who earned the wages of a shoemaker give away as much money as I have all these years?"

The rabbi called all the villagers together and told them the story. "The Miser has lived by the Scriptures, keeping his charity a secret," the rabbi told them. Then they all walked to the grave of The Miser and prayed. And before his own death, the rabbi asked to be buried near the fence, next to the grave of the man known as The Miser.

From the Scripture passage and this story, we can glean many things. Here are just three.

First, all Christians are called to practice the virtue of humility. Humility is a modest estimate of one's own importance. The opposite of humility is arrogance or conceit.

Second, Christian leaders are called to demonstrate humility through the servant-leadership model. The leader devotes self to the service of others, always putting himself or herself second, while putting those he or she serves in first place. Jesus demonstrated this leadership model at the Last Supper when he knelt down and washed the feet of his disciples.

And third, humble leaders can be very effective in the long run. People who are bullies can often get their way in the short term because people are afraid of them. Humble servant leaders, on the other hand, have the ability to change hearts. People are much more likely to truly follow a leader whom they love rather than fear. An excellent example of a servant leader in modern times was Gandhi of India.

As we continue our life journeys this week, it would be a good idea for us to examine our own lives. How do we serve others? How do we practice the virtue of humility in our daily lives?

And that is the good news I have for you on this Twenty-Fifth Sunday in Ordinary Time.

Story source: Anonymous, "The Miser," in William R. White, *Stories for Telling: A Treasury for Christian Storytellers*, Minneapolis, Augsburg Publishing House, 1986, pp. 101-102.

Chapter 49

26th Sunday in Ordinary Time - B
Priorities

Scripture:

- Numbers 11: 25-29
- Psalm 19: 8, 10, 12-13, 14
- James 5: 1-6
- Mark 9: 38-43, 45, 47-48

Today, Catholic Christians celebrate the Twenty-Sixth Sunday in Ordinary Time.

On this day, we hear an amazingly vivid and sharp rebuke of the rich of the world who have not used their wealth wisely. We read from the Letter of James, "Come now, you rich, weep and wail over your impending miseries. Your wealth has rotted away, your clothes have become moth-eaten, your gold and silver have corroded, and that corrosion will be a testimony against you; it will devour your flesh like a fire. You have stored up treasure for the last days. Behold, the wages you withheld from the workers who harvested your fields are crying aloud; and the cries of the harvesters have reached the ears of the Lord of hosts. You have lived on earth in luxury and pleasure; you have fattened your hearts for the day of slaughter" (James 5: 1-5).

One of the primary lessons this passage teaches us is to set our priorities straight. That is what the philosophy professor in the following story tried to teach his students, by way of a creative demonstration.

First, the professor took an empty glass jar and started to fill it with golf balls. When he could not fit any more balls into the jar, he asked the class if the jar was full. They answered, "Yes."

He then picked up a box of pebbles and poured them gently into the jar, shaking the jar a little so that the pebbles could get in between the golf balls. When he could fit no more pebbles, he asked the class if the jar was full. Again, they said, "Yes."

He then picked up a box of sand and began to pour the sand into the jar. The sand filled up all of the spaces in between the pebbles and balls. When no more sand could fit, the students once again agreed the jar was full.

The professor then took two cans of beer and poured them into the jar, effectively filling up all the remaining space.

After doing that, the professor said, "I want you to recognize that this jar represents your life. The golf balls represent the very important things in your life such as your family, health, friends, faith, and passions. If everything else was lost, and only the golf balls remained, your life would be full.

"The pebbles represent other things that matter in your life, things like your job, car, house, and clothes. The sand represents everything else in your life, the things that are truly not important.

"If you fill the jar with sand first, then there would be no room for the golf balls and pebbles. Your life would lack meaning. Therefore, you need to set priorities in your life, filling it with the truly important things. Spend quality time with children. Visit your parents and grandparents more often. Take your spouse on 'date nights.' Expand your mind with new interests. Take time to relax and laugh.

"Take care of the golf balls first – the things that really matter. Do you now see the importance of setting priorities? Everything else is just sand."

One student raised her hand and asked what the beer represented. The professor smiled and said, "I'm glad you asked. The beer just shows you that no matter how full your life may seem, there's always room for a couple of beers with a friend."

This story, taken with the Scripture passage from St. James, illustrates several things that we need to keep in mind. Here are just three.

First, the material world is fleeting. We can take no material thing with us into eternity. Therefore, we need to focus on what counts – our spiritual life. We need to prioritize. Many people spend their whole lives focusing on pleasure, on self-indulgence. What will that get them? Nothing.

Second, James reminds us we are to be honest, especially in dealing with those who rely on our honesty. For example, James condemns those in authority who withhold wages from their workers. Treating workers with dignity and respect is a foundational value in Catholic social teaching. Because of abuse of workers through history, the Catholic Church has insisted that workers have certain rights to be paid an honest wage, have decent working conditions, and have the right to form unions. Likewise, workers must do an honest day's work for an honest day's wage.

And third, we are called to be generous. In the New Testament, we are reminded in many places that the more we have, the more is expected of us (e.g., Luke 12: 48). Because Americans are so blessed with the world's goods, we are called to be people of commensurate generosity. We are called to share and share abundantly with those of the world who have so little. This is not a mere suggestion. It is a Christian commandment.

As we continue our life journeys this week, it would be a good idea to examine our consciences by asking ourselves some probing questions. How do we demonstrate that we understand the fleeting nature of the material world? How do we prioritize our lives? How do we deal with the world of work and the treatment of workers? And how generous are we with our time, talent, and treasure?

And that is the good news I have for you on this Twenty-Sixth Sunday in Ordinary Time.

Story source: Anonymous, "The Importance of Setting Priorities," www. whatyoucanachieve.com, September 27, 2015.

Chapter 50

27th Sunday in Ordinary Time - B
Too Much Togetherness

Scripture:

- Genesis 2: 18-24
- Psalm 128: 1-2, 3, 4-5, 6
- Hebrews 2: 9-11
- Mark 10: 2-16

Today, Catholic Christians celebrate the Twenty-Seventh Sunday in Ordinary Time.

On this day, the Scripture readings tell us of the social nature of human beings, the nobility of marriage, and the preciousness of children. In Scripture, marriage and family are often presented in an idyllic manner. However, we all know that marriage is not always good for the couple, and that families can be dysfunctional and destructive institutions.

In the following story, we hear from a woman who wrote to an advice columnist in the old *Chicago Daily News*. As she pointed out, people in families can often get on each other's nerves even when they love each other. The woman wrote:

> I've heard of the problems newly retired men and their wives face when confronted by too much togetherness, and I was always amused at the way they so often get on each other's nerves. I never thought I'd face such a problem, but it's been two months now, and matters around here are pretty bad.
>
> I ran out of patience that first Monday. There we were, the two of us. Dave busied himself by following me around, inquiring into my household routines. I tried to be pleasant, but my surly nature surfaced when he asked, "Why don't you vacuum all the way under the bed?" I've tried to interest him in any number of activities, with little success. I've even shouted the merits of daytime TV. "What you really need is a job," I told him, knowing he'd never be able to find one at his age.
>
> Yesterday was typical. Dave and I spent the morning together, as always now. He sat looking out the window for a while, sighing intermittently. Then, he came into the kitchen and asked, "When are we having lunch?" This was at 8:30 in the morning! We went, lockstep, to the bedrooms, where he watched me make beds. When he asked, "What should we do now?" I snarled, "How about a duel with sabers?" A lengthy discussion followed of my system of sorting wash. I don't like to sort wash, much less talk about it!

The situation is getting to me. You'd think that someone with so much intelligence, someone I truly love would not be so totally annoying when faced with a change in routine. Ah, well, my problem won't last forever. Next fall, Dave will be in kindergarten.

This amusing story, along with today's Scripture readings, can teach us many things. Here are just three.

First, human beings are social in nature. In the Book of Genesis, for example, we read, "The Lord God said: 'It is not good for the man to be alone. I will make a suitable partner for him'" (Genesis 2: 18).

Because humans are social in nature, Catholic Christianity has developed a rich theology of how we are to interact with other. We know, for example, that we need to treat all people with dignity and respect. We are to serve others, because Christ lives in each of us. We know about the corporal works of mercy and the spiritual works of mercy. We know of many virtues that can only be put into effect when there more than one person is involved. Generosity, for example, needs both a giver and a receiver.

Second, as we read in the Gospel of Mark today, the vows two people make to each other in marriage are sacred. They are a covenant, not merely a contract. In Catholic theology, a covenant is a promise in good times and in bad times. However, there are cases when marriage is so destructive, that it is wise to end it. If you believe you are in such a situation, please see me or another priest. You should not live a life destructive to your spirit.

And third, just as Catholic Christians are to give "preferential option to the poor," we are also called to give special treatment to children. The foundation for the idea that children are extremely precious is seen in today's passage from the Gospel of St. Mark. We read, "And people were bringing children to him that he might touch them. 'Let the children come to me; do not prevent them, for the kingdom of God belongs to such as these. Amen, I say to you, whoever does not accept the kingdom of God like a child will not enter it.' Then he embraced them and blessed them, placing his hands on them" (Mark 10: 13-16).

As we continue our life journeys this week, it would be a good idea to ask ourselves some questions. If we are in a coupled relationship, how to do we show our love to our partner? How could we do better? How do we show special love and attention to children?

And that is the good news I have for you on this Twenty-Seventh Sunday in Ordinary Time.

Story source: Anonymous, "Togetherness," In William J. Bausch, *A World of Stories for Preachers and Teachers,* Mystic, Connecticut, Twenty-Third Publications, 1998, #298, pp. 374-375.

Chapter 51

28th Sunday in Ordinary Time - B
Fr. Casimir Cypher

Scripture:

- Wisdom 7: 7-11
- Psalm 90: 12-13, 14-15, 16-17
- Hebrews 4: 12-13
- Mark 10: 17-30

Today, Catholic Christians celebrate the Twenty-Eighth Sunday in Ordinary Time.

On this day, we hear some intriguing teachings from Jesus in the Gospel of Mark. The context for today's lessons is this. Jesus talks to his disciples about how difficult it is for the rich to enter into the kingdom of God. The disciples were astonished and asked, "Then who can be saved?" (Mark 10: 26). Jesus replied, "For mortals, it is impossible, but not for God; for God all things are possible" (Mark 10: 27).

Then, Peter reminded Jesus that he and the other disciples had given up everything to follow Jesus. He wondered just what the payoff would be. So, Jesus gave the disciples an amazing list of benefits that came with the job of being his follower. He said, "Amen, I say to you, there is no one who has given up house or brothers or sisters or mother or father or children or lands for my sake and for the sake of the gospel who will not receive a hundred times more now in this present age: houses and brothers and sisters and mothers and children and lands, with persecutions, and eternal life in the age to come" (Mark 10: 29-30).

I have always been fascinated by this list of job benefits Jesus gives. First, the list contains positive earthly benefits and ends with the ultimate divine benefit – eternal life. Sandwiched in between the earthly and divine benefits, however, is the promise of persecutions.

Throughout the 2,000-year history of the Catholic Church, we have seen many people who have indeed followed Jesus and who have, sure enough, suffered persecutions. In our own time, for example, we have many examples of men and women who were martyred for the faith. Before he was killed himself, Archbishop Óscar Romero reminded his fellow Catholic Christians in El Salvador of that very thing when he said, "Christ invites us not to fear persecution because, believe me, brothers and sisters, those who are committed to the poor must risk the same fate as the poor, and in El Salvador we know what the fate of the poor signifies: to disappear, to be tortured, to be captive, and to be found dead."

Today, we look at the life of a man of our time who was, indeed, killed for the faith. His name was Michael Cypher, later known in Religious life as Fr. Casimir.

Michael Cypher was born on January 12, 1941 in Medford, Wisconsin. He was the tenth of twelve children of a farm family.

After spending his childhood and teen years in Catholic schools, Michael joined the Conventual Franciscans. As a seminarian, Michael was known for his great kindness, sense of humor, simplicity, and generosity. He loved nature and loved to write.

He graduated from Loyola University in Chicago and was ordained a priest in 1968. In Religious life, his name was Casimir.

After serving as a parish priest in Illinois and California, Fr. Casimir felt called to the missions of Honduras. As a missionary, he went to the Department of Olancho. (A department is like a state.) There, he worked with the poorest of the poor. At the time that Fr. Casimir served in that area of Honduras, almost half of all children died before the age of five. In the missions, he celebrated Mass and other sacraments with the people, ran a parish and school, and served in any way he could. Though his Spanish was far from perfect, the people loved him because they knew he loved them.

Unfortunately, during his time in Honduras, there was great political strife. Though Fr. Casimir was not known for being political, he was a Catholic priest, and as such, the government regarded him as a champion of the poor.

On June 25, 1975, five thousand poor and landless peasants began a six-day "Hunger March" from Olancho to the nation's capital, Tegucigalpa, to demand that the government act on promises it had made on land reforms.

Paramilitary groups that were controlled by wealthy landowners and the Honduran Army moved to stop the march, raided the bishop's residence, and attacked Catholic rectories, as well as any civil institutions associated with the reform movement.

On the day of the march, Fr. Casimir was taking an old truck to the repair shop. When he heard shots coming from the public square, he ran to see what was happening. Many believed that the soldiers mistook him for another priest, although others said that it didn't matter, as all priests were seen as enemies of the state.

He was captured, stripped naked, and beaten. Despite constant humiliation from the authorities, he ran through the square blessing dead bodies of the poor and anointing those still alive. Finally, he, another priest, and some women were taken to a detention facility and sentenced to death. Many people were baked alive. After unspeakable torture, the priests were shot in the head. Fr. Casimir was 34 years old. The priests' dead bodies were thrown into a dry well with live people, dynamited, and then bulldozed to conceal the crime.

With the help of the United States government, the bodies were eventually found and buried. Today, people all over Honduras honor Fr. Casimir in the Cathedral of Gualaco in Olancho.

Though you and I will probably not have the honor of martyrdom, people and circumstances will test our faith. Let's pray we will be ready for the challenges, for as Jesus promised, we will have "life eternal."

And that is the good news I have for you on this Twenty-Eighth Sunday in Ordinary Time.

Story sources:

- *Marytown* (www.marytown.com). No date.
- Rev. Casimir (Michael) Cypher, OFM Conv., Holy Rosary Parish, No date.

Chapter 52

29th Sunday in Ordinary Time - B
Bishop Edward J. Galvin

Scripture:

- Isaiah 53: 10-11
- Psalm 33: 4-5, 18-19, 20 & 22
- Hebrews 4: 14-16
- Mark 10: 35-45

Today, Catholic Christians celebrate the Twenty-Ninth Sunday in Ordinary Time.

This year, we celebrate this day as World Mission Sunday, a day when we remember all of our Catholic missionaries on the front lines. The second collections that are held in churches throughout the United States go to support the 1,100 dioceses of the world that are considered to be "mission dioceses."

Some of the projects of mission dioceses include catechetical programs, education of seminarians, mission work of Religious communities, communication and transportation needs, and the building of chapels and churches, hospitals and clinics, orphanages and schools.

On this special Sunday, we read an interesting command Jesus gave to his disciples. In this selection from St. Mark, we hear that the Zebedee brothers – James and John – had asked Jesus that they be permitted to sit at his right and his left in the world to come. The other disciples, when they learned about the brothers' wishes, were angry with the brothers. Jesus responded that he was not in charge of who was to be located in which part of heaven.

Jesus then gave the disciples an important lesson about leadership when he said, "You know that those who are recognized as rulers over the Gentiles lord it over them, and their great ones make their authority over them felt. But it shall not be so among you. Rather, whoever wishes to be great among you will be your servant; whoever wishes to be first among you will be the slave of all. For the Son of Man did not come to be served but to serve and to give his life as a ransom for many" (Mark 10: 42-45).

Throughout the 2,000-year history of the Catholic Church, many have followed Jesus' servant-leader model of leadership. Today, we look at the life of one such man named Edward J. Galvin.

Edward was born in 1882 on the feast day of St. Columban, November 23, in County Cork, Ireland. As a young boy, he had a desire to be a missionary when he grew up, and this desire never really left him.

He went to the seminary of St. Patrick's College in Maynooth to become a priest of his home Diocese of Cork. He was ordained in 1909.

Unfortunately for Fr. Edward, there was no room for newly ordained priests in the Diocese of Cork at the time, because there were already too many priests. So, with some other newly ordained young men, Edward went to the Diocese of Brooklyn in New York City. There, he served as an associate at Holy Rosary parish. During that time, the desire to be a missionary still burned in his heart. Twice he asked to become a missionary – one time as a missionary to Africa, and another time as a missionary to Arizona. Both times, his offer was rejected.

For some reason, he began to think of China and what it would be like to be a missionary there. Soon, he found himself reading every book about China he could get his hands on. Then one day a Canadian missionary who was working in China came to visit Holy Rosary parish. The missionary, Fr. John Mary Fraser, later founded the Scarboro Missionary Society in Canada.

Fr. Edward asked if Fr. Fraser would take him to China with him, and Fr. Fraser gladly accepted. So, at the age of 29, Fr. Edward sailed to China where he would devote the rest of his life to the Chinese people.

In China, Fr. Edward lived the life of a missionary to the fullest. He was so excited by his life and the great needs of the people, that he invited other Irish priests to come and join him. And little by little, more and more Irish priests come to China. On June 29, 1918, the Holy See approved the Society of St. Columban. This organization was the official missionary society of Ireland, much like Maryknoll is for the United States of America. Soon, the society opened its own seminary to train men for the missions.

By 1920, just eight years after Fr. Edward went to China, the Society of St. Columban comprised 40 priests and 60 seminarians.

In China, Fr. Edward faced every kind of test imaginable: floods, bandits, kidnapping, deaths of fellow missionaries, hunger, civil wars, fires, and other perils. In 1927, he was ordained as Bishop of Hanyang. He faithfully served the people of China until he was expelled from China in 1952 with other Catholic missionaries by the Communist government. He died in Ireland on February 23, 1956.

Bishop Edward Galvin always put his priests and people first, and himself second. If there ever was a person who demonstrated Jesus' servant-leadership model, it was Edward.

William E. Barrett, author of two books that became American movies – *The Lilies of the Field* and *The Left Hand of God* – wrote a magnificent book about Bishop Galvin called *The Red Lacquered Gate*.

As we continue our life journeys this week, it would be a good idea to reflect on the life of Bishop Galvin and those who serve on the front lines in mission territories on our behalf. How often do we pray for these missionaries? How do we support them in other ways?

And that is the good news I have for you on this Twenty-Ninth Sunday in Ordinary Time.

Story sources:

• William E. Barrett, *The Red Lacquered Gate*, New York, Sheed & Ward, 1967.
• Fr. Pat Sayles, "Edward J. Galvin: Trailblazer for God," *Misyon Online*, March-April 2010.

Chapter 53

30th Sunday in Ordinary Time - B
A Change in Dreams

Scripture:

- Jeremiah 31: 7-9
- Psalm 126: 1-2ab, 2cd-3, 4-5, 6
- Hebrews 5: 1-6
- Mark 10: 46-52

Today, Catholic Christians celebrate the Thirtieth Sunday in Ordinary Time.

In today's reading from the Letter to the Hebrews, we are reminded that it is God who chooses people to be priests. The author says, "Every high priest is taken from among men and made their representative before God, to offer gifts and sacrifices for sins. He is able to deal patiently with the ignorant and erring, for he himself is beset by weakness and so, for this reason, must make sin offerings for himself as well as for the people. No one takes this honor upon himself but only when called by God, just as Aaron was" (Hebrews 5: 1-4).

The primary way God calls men to be priests is, I believe, by planting a desire in their hearts to become a priest. However, just because one receives the "call" does not mean that God will eventually choose him. That is what we see in the story of a black boy named Paul who lived in South Africa.

One day, Paul was sitting under a tree lost in thought. He was daydreaming about how wonderful it would be to be an ordained priest. As he was sitting there, a Religious Sister walked by and asked, "Paul, what are you thinking about?" He replied, "Sister, I'm thinking that I would like to be a priest." Sister was favorably impressed, because she knew he was a good boy both at play and at work, and that he attended Mass every day.

When Paul graduated from school, he sought to enter the seminary. Unfortunately, however, the seminary said he must pay 60 pounds. For a poor boy like Paul, 60 pounds was more money than he could even dream of having. So he decided to work and save up the money he needed to enter the seminary.

Although Paul worked on a farm, the pay was very little, especially for a black boy like himself. Therefore, he decided he had to go to work in the Johannesburg gold mines. The mines, in those days, were dangerous places for one's physical health. And, as many young men discovered, they were often dangerous to one's spiritual health, for on their days off the young men often found themselves in the midst of temptations in the big city of Johannesburg.

Paul signed a three-year contract to work in the mines. He endured terrible heat and dampness underground and brutal treatment from the overseers of the mine. However, he persevered and, after three years, he had saved up the 60 pounds needed to get into the seminary.

With the money in his pocket, he went to the Marianhill seminary to seek admission. He told the priest about his desire to enter and how he had worked for three years to get the necessary entry fee. But as he talked to the priest, he kept coughing.

The priest told Paul that before he could enter the seminary, he had to have a physical exam to see if he was okay. Paul did as he was told, and asked the physician to send the report to the priest at the seminary.

When Paul returned to the seminary, the priest told him that his physical exam showed he had miner's tuberculosis and had only one or two years to live. When Paul first heard the news, he broke down sobbing and coughing. Then, he said, "I was afraid of that."

The kind priest said, "Paul, nobody knows how God works in these things. He obviously does not call you to be a priest. I would suggest you keep the money you saved, buy a little plot of land here, and live happily close to the mission."

Paul replied, "No, Father, that isn't what I worked for. I wanted to be a priest. If I can't be one myself, perhaps some other boy can be one for me. You will find some boy who will make a good priest. Take the money, I don't want it, give it to him. I'm going back to the mines. It doesn't matter when I die. If I live another few years, I might save enough for another boy too."

Paul did go back to the mines. In 1935, according to the Catholic paper of that year, he was still working in the mines and praying that God would keep him alive a little bit longer to get another few pounds for his second priest.

This incredibly inspirational story, coupled with today's reading from the Letter to the Hebrews, reminds us of several things.

First, God's ways are not our ways, and God's thoughts are not our thoughts. It is pure folly to figure out God's plan for the universe.

Second, we know that "many are called but few are chosen" (Matthew 22: 14). This especially applies, I believe, to the ordained priesthood.

And third, we need resiliency in our life journey, for we never how where the journey will take us. Resiliency, here, refers to being able to recover or bounce back from adversity. Like Paul in this story, we too must be ready for "Plan B" – or "Plan C" or whatever - when "Plan A" does not work out.

As we continue our life journeys this week, it would be a good idea to reflect on our own life journeys. How often did we think God wanted us to do one thing, but in actuality, he called us to something else? How have we been called to show resiliency on our life journeys?

And that is the good news I have for you on this Thirtieth Sunday in Ordinary Time.

Story source: F.H. Drinkwater, "Vocation to the Priesthood," in *Catechism Stories*, American Authors Press, 1939, pp. 367-368.

Chapter 54

31st Sunday in Ordinary Time - B
The Faith on One Foot

Scripture:

- Deuteronomy 6: 2-6
- Psalm 18: 2-3a, 3bc-4, 47 & 51ab
- Hebrews 7: 23-28
- Mark 12: 28b-34

Today, Catholic Christians celebrate the Thirty-First Sunday in Ordinary Time.

On this day, in the Gospel of Mark, Jesus teaches his disciples the very foundation on which we, as his followers, must stand in our behavior. This teaching is called the triple love command of Jesus. When a scribe asked Jesus which of all of the commandments was the greatest, Jesus answered, "The first is this: Hear, O Israel! The Lord our God is Lord alone! You shall love the Lord your God with all your heart, with all your soul, with all your mind, and with all your strength. The second is this: you shall love your neighbor as yourself. There is no other commandment greater than these" (Mark 12: 29-31).

When looking at this teaching, it is good to keep a couple of things in mind. First, Jesus did not "invent" the triple love command. We find the first part of the command – to love God above all – in the Book of Deuteronomy (6: 4-5). And we find the second part of the command in Leviticus (19:18). Second, we need to keep in mind that the second part of the triple command is that we should love ourselves. Often, even preachers skip that part of the triple love command of Jesus when they focus exclusively on the love of God and neighbor. We should never forget to treasure self, for our self is God's gift to us.

In the following story by Fr. Jim Mazzone, we encounter a young man who put some priests to a test. Two of them failed the test, while the third passed.

There was once an oddly dressed young man who came into a new town carrying a little suitcase. The young man walked into the center of town and spun himself around a couple of times and then looked up at the skyline. After fixing his eyes on the steeple of a church, he went to the priest's house next to the church. When he was invited in, he explained that he was new in town and wanted to join a church. The young man continued by saying, "However, before joining your church, I'd like you to teach me the whole faith while I stand on one foot." Then, the man stood on just one foot. The priest thought the man was crazy and ushered him right out the door.

The young man then went into the center of town again, twirled himself around once again, and looked up at the skyline to see a different church steeple. After walking to the second priest's house, he made the same request and stood on one foot. The priest immediately ushered him to the door, believing that he was crazy.

The young man, for a third time, went to the center of town, spun himself around, and found a third church steeple. When he met the priest of this third church, he repeated his desire to join a church and his desire to be taught the entire faith while standing on one foot. As he stood on one foot, the kind and wise priest said, "Love God and love your neighbor as you love yourself. The rest is all commentary." At that, the young man settled in the town, joined the church, and became one of the most active and faithful lay ministers the church had ever seen.

Now on the surface, the triple love command seems to be very easy to comprehend. After all, we think, it's only three little parts: love God, love neighbor, and love self. What could be easier than that?

As we know, though, there are frequently many temptations that come our way to persuade us to not love God, or our neighbor, or our self. Let's look at each of these three commands.

First, we are to love God above all else. When many people hear this, they begin looking at rules and commandments of God to see if they are obeying them. And that is a good way to begin. I know many people – including priests – who use the Jewish "10 Commandments" as the basis of the Examination of Conscience before celebrating the Sacrament of Reconciliation. Others, like me, use the Triple Love Command of Jesus.

Second, we are to love our neighbor. To fully appreciate this part of the triple love command, however, we need to define "love." The best definition I have heard of the concept of love is to wish the best for a person – either self or another. When we truly grasp that concept, we are led to the amazing rich and fascinating world of virtues. We are also led, though, to the world of vices. When examining on how charitable or generous or forgiving we are, we can't help but examine our behavior in relation to others. These virtues do not exist in a vacuum.

And third, we are to love our self. For many people, this is the most difficult part of the triple love commandment. In the realm of mistakes, for example, many people are very quick to forgive others, and they are confident in God's forgiveness. However, they are often so hard on themselves that they walk through the world with a figurative baseball bat continually hitting themselves over the head with it. Others fail to care for their bodies, abusing it with harmful substances, a lack of exercise, inadequate sleep, or poor nutrition. Others fail to develop the talents the God gave them to grow and flourish and continually move to become better people.

As we continue our life journeys this week, it would be a good idea to reflect on how we live the triple love command of Jesus Christ. How are we doing putting God first in our lives? How do we love our neighbor? How do we love our self?

And that is the good news I have for you on this Thirty-First Sunday of Ordinary Time.

Story source: Fr. Jim Mazzone. From his homily of the 31ˢᵗ Sunday of Ordinary Time, Cycle B. Catholic Lectionary Homilies. N.D.

Chapter 55

32nd Sunday in Ordinary Time - B
Bobby's Valentines

Scripture:

- 1 Kings 17: 10-16
- Psalm 146: 6c-7, 8-9a, 9bc-10
- Hebrews 9: 24-28
- Mark 12: 38-44

Today, Catholic Christians celebrate the Thirty-Second Sunday in Ordinary Time. On this day, we hear some important aspects of the nature of giving.

In the First Book of Kings, we hear about a poor widow. As she was gathering some sticks for a cook fire, the prophet Elijah called out to her and asked her if she would bring him a cup of water. As she went to get it, he also asked for some bread. The poor widow, however, told the prophet she barely had enough food for herself and her son. Elijah, however, told her not to worry, for God would provide.

The widow obeyed and brought Elijah a little cake she had made. And as a result of her generosity, God provided the widow and her son enough food for a year (1 Kings 17: 10-16).

In the gospel selection from St. Mark, we hear about Jesus watching people put money into the temple's treasury. After observing for a while, he called over his disciples and said how impressed he was with a widow who, from her poverty, had contributed all she had, her whole livelihood. This pleased him much more than the large sums of money that some people contributed, because they had contributed from their surplus wealth (Mark 12: 41-44).

Before discussing some of the things we can learn from today's Scripture lessons on giving, let's look at the following story by Sonny Salsbury that gives us more insight into the nature of giving.

There was once a special education boy named Bobby. He was smart enough to be in a regular classroom, but he was noticeably different from the other children. His classmates frequently teased him because he was different, but he never seemed to mind. Every afternoon at the end of the school day, Bobby's mother would look out her window to see the kids coming from school. Every day, she would see groups of kids laughing and joking together – all except Bobby. He was always walking behind the groups by himself. It was obvious that the other children felt uncomfortable around Bobby and, therefore, shunned him.

One day, Bobby burst into the kitchen after school, filled with joy and enthusiasm. He said, "Mom, guess what? Valentine's Day is just two weeks away, and our teacher said we could make valentines and give them to the other kids in our class!"

His mother's heart sank as she imagined yet another opportunity for Bobby to be excluded. Bobby, though, focused on his plans for Valentine's

Day and said, "Mom, I'm going to make a valentine for every person in my class!"

"That's nice, Bobby" replied Bobby's mother. She was fighting back tears.

Over the next two weeks, Bobby worked every afternoon on valentines for his classmates. They were truly labors of love. When the big day finally came, Bobby was so excited that he couldn't even eat breakfast. He was also a little worried. He was afraid that he might have forgotten to make a valentine for someone in his class.

As the day wore on, Bobby's mother made a fresh batch of cookies. She mentally prepared herself to comfort her son when he returned home brokenhearted from the valentine exchange. She believed he would be crushed when he did not receive even a single valentine.

That afternoon, as Bobby's mother looked out the window, she saw the groups of neighborhood kids laughing and talking as always. And as always, Bobby was walking by himself a half a block behind them.

Much to her surprise, when Bobby came through the door, he had a huge smile on his face. She asked, "What is it, Bobby? How did it go at school?"

Bobby, with a shout of pure joy, said, "Guess what, Mom! I didn't miss a single kid! Not a single one!"

This story and the Scriptures can teach us many things about the nature of giving from a Biblical perspective. Here are just three.

First, we are to be generous to others. Not only is generosity a very important virtue, it shows that we understand the second part of the triple love commandment, that is, to love others.

When we are generous with our blessings, we also need to be prudent and wise. We need to remember the third part of the triple love commandment, that is, that we are also to love ourselves. Thus, we always need to keep enough of our blessings to live a life that does not cause burdens to others.

Second, giving often requires us to take a "leap of faith." That is what the widow had to do when she gave the prophet Elijah food. You and I are often asked to make financial gifts to worthy things such as a capital campaign for our parish or the Bishop's Annual Appeal or a visiting missionary. We do not know what the future holds for us, but we give because we know that God will take care of us.

And third, we read in many parts of the New and Old Testament that God will bless us when we are generous. That is exactly what happened to the poor widow who made a cake for the prophet Elijah. God blessed her generosity by providing enough food for her and her son for a full year.
We are not to give just to gain recognition. Bobby, in our story, showed that. He was so focused on giving, that it never dawned on him to consider receiving. Thus, we are to give because it is the right thing to do as a follower of Jesus Christ.

As we continue our life journeys this week, it would be a good idea to reflect on generosity. How important is that virtue to us? How do we show this virtue by our own giving? How has God blessed us as a result of our generosity?

And that is the good news I have for you on this Thirty-Second Sunday in Ordinary Time.

Story source: Sonny Salsbury, "Bobby's Valentines," in Wayne Rice (Ed.), *Hot Illustrations for Youth Talks 4*, Grand Rapids, Michigan, Youth Specialties/Zondervan, 2001, pp. 47-48.

Chapter 56

33rd Sunday in Ordinary Time - B
When Prophecy Fails

_____

Scripture:

_____

- Daniel 12: 1-3
- Psalm 16: 5 & 8, 9-10, 11
- Hebrews 10: 11-14, 18
- Mark 13: 24-32

Today, Catholic Christians celebrate the Thirty-Third Sunday in Ordinary Time. Because this is the second-to-the-last Sunday of the Church Year, it is not surprising that the Scripture readings focus on the end times.

In the Book of Daniel, for example, we hear about the rise of a prince named Michael and the awakening of the dead. And in the Gospel of Mark, we hear Jesus tell us about "the Son of Man coming in the clouds" (Mark 13: 26). Though these passages talk about what it might be like at the end of time in terms of signs, Jesus reminds us that nobody will know when this "end of time" will occur. Specifically, Jesus says, "But of that day or hour, no one knows, neither the angels in heaven, nor the Son, but only the Father" (Mark 13: 32).

Now we know that often Jesus speaks in parables that are unclear and open to various interpretations. But about knowing when the end times will come, he is crystal clear: nobody knows, not even him. Nevertheless, through the ages, there have always been people who refuse to believe Jesus. They are convinced they have special knowledge allowing them to know when the end of the world will come.

Sometimes, people who believe they know when the end times will occur continue to believe in this knowledge, even when the date and time they predicted for the end of the world came and went, and the world continued as always. That is what we see in the very interesting study by University of Iowa social psychologist Leon Festinger and his associates. Their study, called *When Prophecy Fails*, is important to us in religion, for it gives us some insight into the nature of beliefs.

Dr. Festinger and colleagues decided to study a group that believed it has special knowledge that the world was coming to an end. Festinger wondered what would happen to this group when their prophecy failed.

Dorothy Martin, a Chicago housewife, founded this group. She had experimented with a phenomenon called "automatic writing," the idea that certain people can produce writings totally free from their own consciousness. Dorothy Martin studied Dianetics, a movement created by science-fiction author L. Ron Hubbard. This movement led to the establishment of the Church of Scientology.

Dorothy Martin claimed that she had received a message from a fictional planet called Clarion. The message said that the world would end in a great flood before dawn on December 21, 1954. Fortunately, however, a flying saucer would pick up Dorothy Martin and her followers to save them in time. The group members left their jobs, colleges, and spouses. They gave away their money and possessions and prepared to board the flying saucer.

Well, needless to say, December 21, 1954 came and went, and the world did not end. So, what happened to the group and their beliefs? That is what Dr. Festinger wanted to know.

He discovered that despite the failure of the prophecy, many people of Dorothy Martin's group continued to believe they had special knowledge of the end times.

Dr. Festinger found that the people whose beliefs were least shaken were people who had shown great commitment to the beliefs. For example, people who had sold everything were more likely to hold onto their beliefs than people who did not give up anything. Also, people who surrounded themselves exclusively with people who believed as they did were more likely to hold onto their beliefs.

From the Scripture passages and the scientific study of failed prophecy, we can learn many things. Here are just three.

First, we do not know when the end of time – or the Second Coming of Jesus – will be. That is not for us to know. When we hear about "signs" such as war, famine, earthquakes, and other things, we should not jump to the conclusion that they indicate the end of the world. We know that such "signs" have been with us throughout human history. In short, we should believe Jesus when he said, "nobody knows."

Second, though the Catholic Church teaches that "divine revelation" has already been given to us, the Church is still "unpacking" this revelation. That is why we have fields such as Bible Studies and Theology. In studying Scripture we are like prospectors looking for nuggets of gold that we might have missed.

And third, from Festinger's study, we saw that people who were most firmly rooted in their belief system were those who surrounded themselves with those who held the same beliefs. This finding can lead us into both good and bad conclusions. It is fine to have close friends who believe as we do. That helps strengthen our faith. However, it can also lead some to become close-minded and actually hostile towards their fellow human beings.

As we continue our life journeys this week, it would be a good idea to reflect on our beliefs. How do we strive to be good followers of Jesus? How do we prepare ourselves every day for our transition from this life to the next?

And that is the good news I have for you on this Thirty-Third Sunday in Ordinary Time.

Story source: Festinger, Leon; Henry W. Riecken; Stanley Schachter,), *When Prophecy Fails: A Social and Psychological Study of a Modern Group that Predicted the Destruction of the World*, University of Minnesota Press, 1955.

Chapter 57

Christ the King - B
The Magical City

Scripture:

- Daniel 7: 13-14
- Psalm 93: 1ab, 1c-2, 5
- Revelation 1: 5-8
- John 18: 33b-37

Today, Catholic Christians celebrate the last Sunday of the Church Year, officially called the Feast of Our Lord Jesus Christ, King of the Universe - more commonly called Christ the King.

Because so many Catholic Christian stories always have a romantic or "happily ever after" ending, it is quite fitting that we should end the Church Year with the idea that Jesus rules over the universe forever. What could be more awesome than that?

On this day, we hear Jesus telling the Roman authorities a little bit about his kingdom. He says, in the Gospel of John, "My kingdom does not belong to this world. If my kingdom did belong to this world, my attendants would be fighting to keep me from being handed over to the Jews. But as it is, my kingdom is not here" (John 18: 36).

Now, although Jesus' kingdom is in heaven, Catholic Christians have always taught that the kingdom, in its primitive and imperfect way, begins here on Earth.

We believe that God puts us on Earth, gives us many gifts, and then expects us to do our part to build up the heavenly kingdom on Earth. Unfortunately, some people are not satisfied. They are the folks who always believe that the "grass is greener on the other side of the fence." That is what we see in the following story called "The Magical City."

There was once a man who had become weary of his life. He was always tired, and he had no joy. He believed that in order to find happiness, he would have to move to a better place, a place where he could grow and flourish and be filled with energy and joy.

So, one day, he decided to leave his ancestral village and travel to find a perfect city, a Magical City. In this Magical City, he was convinced that he his life would be renewed, and where everything would be fresh and exciting and joyful. So off he went with a little knapsack.

After walking for a few days, he found himself deep in a forest. He settled down under a pine tree for the night, took out some food from his knapsack, and had a bite to eat. Before going to sleep, he carefully took off his shoes and pointed them in the new direction in which he was heading.

During the night, however, a jokester came by while he slept and turned his shoes around. When the man woke up the next morning, he carefully stepped into his shoes and continued on to the Magical City.

After a few days, he came to the Magical City. He was surprised that it was not as large as he had imagined it would be. In fact, is looked rather familiar. He found a familiar street, knocked on a familiar door, and met a familiar family there. And he lived in his ancestral town for the rest of his life – full of joy and energy and a sense of purpose.

This story, coupled with the readings of Scripture and teachings of the Church, can teach us many things. Here are just three.

First, although the "kingdom" that Jesus spoke of is heaven, for human beings this kingdom begins on Earth. In the Catholic Christian worldview, what we call "The Church" is actually a collection of people in various levels of the kingdom, each having a head anointed by God.

In this life, the Church has individuals and families. The family is often called the "domestic church" and is headed by parents. The second level of the Church is the parish, headed by a pastor. The third level of the Church is a diocese, headed by a bishop. The fourth level is the whole Church on Earth headed by the Bishop of Rome, also called the pope. And in the next life, Jesus is not only the head of what is called the "Church Triumphant," but also the entire Church – on Earth and in Heaven.

Second, Catholic Christians believe that the kingdom of God starts on Earth, and it is our job to help build it up. We do this by living out the triple love command of Jesus – to love God, to love our neighbors, as we love ourselves.

To build up the kingdom on Earth, God gives us many gifts. We are to be thankful for our gifts, develop them, and then share them abundantly with those who have little. For example, we build up the kingdom on Earth when we strive to eliminate poverty and prejudice and discrimination. We build the kingdom when we care for the sick, visit the imprisoned, and try to find cures for diseases. We build the kingdom when we try to provide employment for all who want it, and then provide workplaces that affirm the dignity of the human person.

And third, we need to "bloom where we are planted." Many people spend their whole lives searching for a "magical city." They roam the planet in search of happiness, trying to escape from misery. These people don't grasp that their boredom or sadness or unfulfillment is not because of their physical location. Rather, it is because of a defeated attitude and a spiritual void. They try to find happiness and joy by searching for a "geographical cure" to their problems, but as they find out, they take their biggest problem with them wherever they go – themselves.

As we continue our life journeys on this final week of the Church Year, let's look closely at our lives. How are we doing our part to build up the kingdom of God here on Earth?

And that is the good news I have for you on this Feast of Christ the King.

Story source: Anonymous, "The Magical City," in William J. Bausch, *A World of Stories for Preachers and Teachers*, Mystic, Connecticut, Twenty-Third Publications, 1998, #157, pp. 294-295.

Made in the USA
San Bernardino, CA
20 August 2016